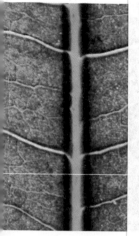

HTML5
and CSS3

Prentice Hall
is an imprint of

PEARSON

Harlow, England • London • New Yor[...] [...]ong
Tokyo • Seoul • Taipei • New Delhi • [...] [...]ilan

D0510347

DUDLEY PUBLIC
LIBRARIES

000000502322	
Bertrams	23/11/2011
006.74	£11.99
	ST

PEARSON EDUCATION LIMITED

Edinburgh Gate
Harlow CM20 2JE
Tel: +44 (0)1279 623623
Fax: +44 (0)1279 431059
Website: www.pearson.com/uk

First published in Great Britain in 2012

© Josh Hill 2012

The right of Josh Hill to be identified as author of this work has been asserted
by him in accordance with the Copyright, Designs and Patents Act 1988.

Pearson Education is not responsible for the content of third-party internet sites.

ISBN: 978-0-273-76258-4

British Library Cataloguing-in-Publication Data
A catalogue record for this book is available from the British Library

Library of Congress Cataloging-in-Publication Data
A catalog record for this book is available from the Library of Congress

All rights reserved. No part of this publication may be reproduced, stored in a retrieval
system, or transmitted in any form or by any means, electronic, mechanical, photocopying,
recording or otherwise, without either the prior written permission of the publisher
or a licence permitting restricted copying in the United Kingdom issued by the
Copyright Licensing Agency Ltd, Saffron House, 6–10 Kirby Street, London EC1N 8TS.
This book may not be lent, resold, hired out or otherwise disposed of by way of trade in
any form of binding or cover other than that in which it is published without the prior
consent of the publisher.

10 9 8 7 6 5 4 3 2 1
15 14 13 12 11

Designed by pentacorbig, High Wycombe
Cover image Cool R, 2011. Used under licence from Shutterstock.com
Typeset in 11/14 pt ITC Stone Sans by 30
Printed and bound by Rotolito Lombarda, Italy

HTML5 and CSS3

in Simple steps

Josh Hill

Use your computer with confidence

Get to grips with practical computing tasks with minimal time, fuss and bother.

In Simple Steps guides guarantee immediate results. They tell you everything you need to know on a specific application; from the most essential tasks to master, to every activity you'll want to accomplish, through to solving the most common problems you'll encounter.

Helpful features

To build your confidence and help you to get the most out of your computer, practical hints, tips and shortcuts feature on every page:

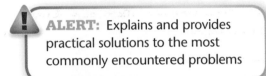 **ALERT:** Explains and provides practical solutions to the most commonly encountered problems

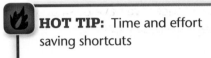 **HOT TIP:** Time and effort saving shortcuts

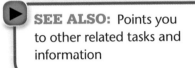 **SEE ALSO:** Points you to other related tasks and information

 **DID YOU KNOW?** Additional features to explore

WHAT DOES THIS MEAN?
Jargon and technical terms explained in plain English

Practical. Simple. Fast.

Author's acknowledgements:

I'd like to thank my wife Vanessa for her hard work, dedication to this project and to me, and for her diligence in keeping me on track. Thank you, love.

I'd also like to thank my agent Neil Salkind from The Salkind Agency, without whom this work wouldn't have been possible, and Steve and the team at Pearson for their patience in working things through with me.

Publisher's acknowledgements:

We are grateful to the following for permission to reproduce copyright material:

Screenshots on pages 10, 17, 18, 120 and 220 from www.veign.com; screenshots on pages 23 and 121 from http://www.css3.info; screenshot on page 141 from http://www.colorschemer.com/online.html; screenshot on page 142 from http://www.december.com/html/spec/color.html, courtesy of december.com.

In some instances we have been unable to trace the owners of copyright material, and we would appreciate any information that would enable us to do so.

Contents at a glance

Top 10 HTML5 and CSS3 Problems Solved

Contents

Top 10 HTML5 and CSS3 Tips

1 Steps before you begin

2 Structuring documents with HTML5

3 Using HTML text markup tags

6 Working with HTML forms and attributes

7 Using more HTML input controls

8 Specifying CSS styles

9 Setting borders and colours with CSS

10 Formatting fonts and text with CSS

11 Controlling white space

12 Sizing elements with CSS

13 Positioning elements with CSS

14 Formatting tables with CSS

Top 10 HTML5 and CSS3 Problems Solved

Top 10 HTML5 and CSS3 Tips

Tip 1: Copy and paste is your friend!

Most text editors have a copy and paste feature. During your web design experience you will encounter situations where it's necessary to repeat markup, whether you're generating a series of elements or a series of controls for a web form. Using copy and paste is the fastest and easiest way to get the markup done.

1 Open the HTML document or the CSS3 style sheet in your text editor.

2 Find the code you need to repeat using the Search or Find feature of the editor.

3 Highlight the line or lines you need to duplicate with your mouse cursor.

4 Copy the highlighted material to the clipboard (keystrokes Ctrl + C or use the Copy command from your text editor).

5 Locate the cursor in the place you want to place the duplicated markup.

6 Paste the copied lines into the new location and edit as necessary.

? DID YOU KNOW?

The keystrokes Ctrl + C are a standard Windows convention and work in most Windows-compliant programs to copy highlighted material to the Windows clipboard. The Copy command in individual text editing software programs, however, may have different images on the button. Almost all of them have the command on the menu set, and in general the Copy command is on the Edit menu.

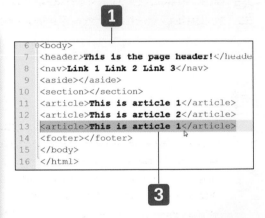

```
 6  <body>
 7  <header>This is the page header!</heade
 8  <nav>Link 1 Link 2 Link 3</nav>
 9  <aside></aside>
10  <section></section>
11  <article>This is article 1</article>
12  <article>This is article 2</article>
13  <article>This is article 1</article>
14  <footer></footer>
15  </body>
16  </html>
```

 HOT TIP: It's faster and easier to paste a duplicate element and change attributes such as id and name rather than re-typing all the markup.

Tip 2: Use a text and code editor to do markup

Markup – or code of any kind for that matter – can become monotonous and hard to read when doing a lot of work. Use of a text editor which colours markup and code can help clarify the lines and assist with distinguishing what on the page is what.

1 Open a web browser to Google's search engine, or the search engine of your choice.

2 Type in the search term 'free colour-coded text editors' and run the query.

3 Find the text editor which seems to best suit your needs; for this book I used Notepad++ exclusively.

4 Download and install the text editor according to the creator instructions.

? **DID YOU KNOW?**

While Notepad++, the text editor used for all the text editing screen captures in this book, is a powerful and free text editor which provides colour-coding capability, there are several others available. Some are freeware, meaning they are free for download and use without charge, and others are commercial software which require you to purchase a licence agreement. Pick the software package which suits your needs best and find out as much as you can about it so you can use it effectively.

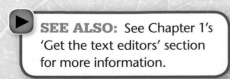

SEE ALSO: See Chapter 1's 'Get the text editors' section for more information.

Tip 3: Test markup in several browsers

Relying on a single browser to view your markup will lead to problems. In just two short years, Google Chrome went from its first version to version 11 (at the time of writing). The world of Internet browsers changes rapidly, with new releases coming as fast as every six weeks sometimes. Some will offer support, others don't, and new releases and updates bring additional support.

1 Download the latest version of Google Chrome from http://www.google.com/chrome.

2 Navigate to http://www.apple.com/safari/ and download Apple's Safari browser.

3 Download Opera's latest Internet browser by going to http://www.opera.com/.

4 Get the latest version of Internet Explorer from http://www.microsoft.com/ and by clicking the Downloads link.

5 Mozilla's Firefox browser is available from http://www.mozilla.com/ – follow the download link there.

6 If you're interested, you can search with your favourite search engine for 'Internet browsers' and find more.

 HOT TIP: While it's always a good idea to make your markup as standard compliant as possible, not all browsers support all features of either HTML5 or CSS3. The best, most browser-friendly solution for some things may actually be to use an older solution from earlier versions of both markup languages.

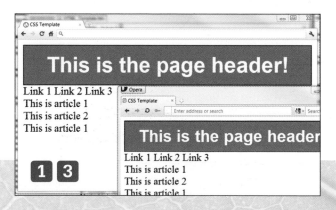

 DID YOU KNOW?

Almost all the screen captures for this book were made using Google Chrome, and the remainder were done with the Opera browser version 11.50. Testing your markup in multiple browsers may be time consuming and tedious, but it will also reveal weaknesses in your code.

Tip 4: Bookmark a good HTML validator

HTML and CSS3 have standards, and the more the markup you've written adheres to those standards, the better the chances are your web pages will look outstanding in all browsers. While validation in CSS is considered less critical, it doesn't hurt to have CSS3 code validated.

1 Open a web browser window.

2 Go to http://validator.w3.org and bookmark the W3C's Markup Validation Service tool for HTML (and other technologies).

3 Go to http://jigsaw.w3.org/css-validator/ and bookmark the CSS Validation Service tool there as well.

4 Do a search with your favourite search engine for other HTML5 and CSS3 validators.

ALERT: Some tools only validate certain markup, so be sure you have the right tool for the job available.

5 Bookmark as many as you feel necessary.

? DID YOU KNOW?
Some validators are extremely experimental. If you use one, realise it may not be the best choice and probably shouldn't be your only tool for validation.

Tip 5: Create an HTML structural document template

This book has you create an HTML document every time you work an exercise, but a faster and easier way to do it is to create a template once and use it for all the tasks as you need them. The HTML document template contains at least one of all the basic HTML structural elements so you have a ready-to-go basic document you can alter as needed. In actual practice this will serve you well as a jumping-off point for building websites by hand.

1 Open a new document in your text editor and save it with the name 'HTML Template.html'.

2 Add the `<!DOCTYPE html>` declaration on the first line at the top of the page.

3 Add the `<html>` element after the declaration.

4 Inside the `<head>` element, add a `<title>` element and `<link />` tag.

5 After the `<head>` tag, add the `<body>` tag inside the `<html>` tag.

6 Add the `<header>`, `<nav>`, `<aside>`, `<section>`, `<article>` and `<footer>` elements in the `<body>` element.

7 Save the template and close it.

SEE ALSO: See Chapter 2, 'Structuring documents with HTML5' for further information on these structural elements.

ALERT: When you open this HTML document using a web browser, nothing will be visible. Don't panic: there is no content on the element. If you'd like, add text as a placeholder for those elements to help you visually locate them.

? DID YOU KNOW?
An HTML document only lays out the basic structure of the web page. While some formatting capabilities exist, formatting is best left to CSS.

```
HTML_Template.htm        1
 1    <!DOCTYPE html>     2
 2   <html>           3
 3   <head>
 4    <title></title>        4
 5    <link />
 6    </head>       5
 7   <body>
 8    <header>This is the page header!</header>
 9    <nav>Link 1 Link 2 Link 3</nav>
10    <aside></aside>       6
11    <section></section>
12    <article>This is article 1</article>
13    <footer></footer>
14    </body>
15    </html>
16
```

Tip 6: Add comments to your code

No matter how experienced a 'code-monkey' you might be, the use of comments to annotate your markup will help with understanding the purpose for the choices made. They can serve as reminders for later reference, or they can serve as notes for others who may be working with the code.

1 Open your HTML template in your text editor and save it with a new name.

2 In the `<body>` element, add an HTML comment starting marker (`<!--`) in front of the `<nav>` element.

3 Add the closing marker (`-->`) after the `</nav>` closing tag.

4 Save the HTML document.

5 Launch the HTML file in your web browser.

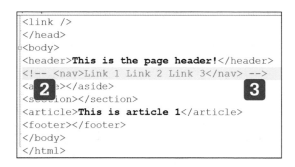

```
<link />
</head>
<body>
<header>This is the page header!</header>
<!-- <nav>Link 1 Link 2 Link 3</nav> -->
<aside></aside>
<section></section>
<article>This is article 1</article>
<footer></footer>
</body>
</html>
```

? **DID YOU KNOW?**
The CSS style sheets created for the exercises in this book may not be long enough to warrant comments, but it's good practice to learn regardless. Comments in CSS are a slash followed by the asterisk (/*) for a start tag, and an asterisk followed by a slash for the end tag (*/). As with HTML comments, be sure to close the comment with an end tag or all the lines following the comment start tag will be commented out.

! **ALERT:** Be careful to close the comment with an end marker, or all the markup will be removed from your document!

Tip 7: Group CSS selectors to apply formatting to multiple elements

If you know, for example, that all headings on a page will receive a specific type of formatting, you can group the selectors together on the same line before the declaration. This makes the coding more efficient and saves time, too. Put all the selectors on the same line separated by commas.

1 Create a new style sheet with your text editor and name it style.css.

2 Grouping selectors, create a declaration to set the `<header>` and `<nav>` element background colours to a light grey: background-color: #CCCCCC;

3 Save the style sheet and close it.

4 Open the HTML template in your text editor and save it with a new name.

5 If necessary, add a `<link />` tag with the href attribute set to the style.css file you've just made.

6 Save the HTML document again and launch it in your web browser. Note the header colour.

> ▶ **SEE ALSO:** See Chapter 9, 'Setting borders and colours with CSS' for more information on specifying colours.

? DID YOU KNOW?

You can use shorthand to specify CSS colours. For instance, if the digits appear in sets of two, such as #334455, you can use only the first, third and fifth digits to specify the same colour. So #345 is the same colour as #334455, or in our example, #CCC is the same colour as #CCCCCC.

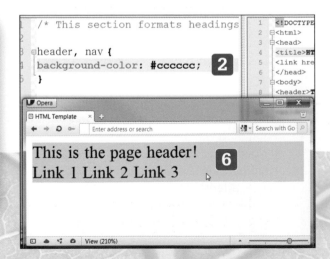

6

Tip 8: View the page source of a website from your browser

Just because you didn't write the code doesn't mean you can't look at it. When you find an especially appealing web page, you can see how the author(s) created the effects you like by opening the page source and viewing it. Emulating the same solutions on your web page can be as simple as checking out how someone else did it first.

1 Open http://w3.org/ in your web browser.

2 Once the page fully loads, hit the Ctrl + U keystroke combination to open the view source window.

3 Explore the solution you'd like to see and examine the code.

4 Copy the source code to your text editor to customise it.

 DID YOU KNOW?
Mozilla SeaMonkey is a web browser with enhancements for web developers and designers. A separate window, called the composer, is an HTML source code editor. It has buttons, command menus and drop-down lists with command sets specific to HTML document creation.

HOT TIP: Ctrl + U will open the page source for viewing in Mozilla Firefox, Google Chrome and Opera browsers.

Tip 9: Use CSS shorthand declarations to set properties

CSS provides longhand and shorthand methods for declaring many properties where individual attributes or aspects of an element can be manipulated. Fonts, borders, margins, padding and others have multiple property declarations for their various portions, such as font weight and style, or top and bottom borders. Using CSS shorthand property declarations makes setting several values faster and cleaner than setting them individually.

1 The font shorthand property sets properties for the individual declarations font-weight, font-style, font-variant, font-size, line-height and font-family.

2 The background declaration covers settings for background-color, background-image, background-repeat, background-attachment and background-position properties.

3 Use the margin declaration to set the properties for margin-top, margin-right, margin-bottom and margin-left declarations.

4 Use the padding declaration to set the padding-top, padding-right, padding-bottom and padding-left properties.

? **DID YOU KNOW?**

This is only a partial sampling of the shorthand property declarations available. There are many resources available online for more information, or use the quick reference guide for CSS3 (see Chapter 1's 'Download a CSS3 quick reference guide' section for details on downloading the quick reference guide).

! **ALERT:** Be sure to consult the documentation for each declaration so the properties are set in the correct order in the declaration, or you may get unexpected results!

BACKGROUND	
background	background-image
	background-position
	background-size
	background-repeat
	background-attachment
	background-origin
	background-clip
	background-color

An example of CSS shorthand declarations, with the property settings possible

Tip 10: Remove browser default settings before writing CSS code

In order to ensure you aren't starting out fighting with browser default settings for margins, padding and border settings, it's good practice to clean up those things before you begin writing CSS code. Setting borders, margins and padding to zero values before you begin lets you start with a blank canvas so you can create the CSS formatting you want without interference.

1 Create a new style.css file with your text editor.

2 Add a grouped selector declaration for the html, body and header properties.

3 Set the margin, padding and border attributes to zero for all of them.

4 Save the style sheet and close it.

5 Open your HTML template in your text editor and add a `<link />` tag with the href attribute set to the style sheet you've just created.

6 Save the HTML document with a new name, then open it in your web browser.

? **DID YOU KNOW?**

Removing the margin, padding and border settings ensures the CSS styles you apply won't be competing with, or layered with, any browser defaults which might exist. While not a necessary step, it's one of the 'best practice' steps which set professional web designers apart from amateurs.

HOT TIP: Be sure to use the principles in this tip for any HTML elements you're going to be working with.

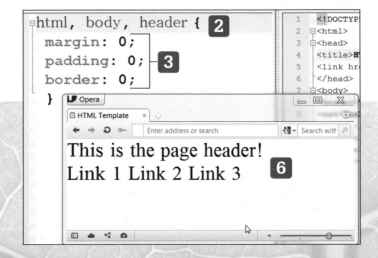

1 Steps before you begin

Introduction

HTML stands for Hyper Text Markup Language. HTML is not a computer programming language but a document markup language. HTML is a set of instructions for the web browser. Instructions, or tags, are placed around text so Internet browsers know how to display the text on screen.

HTML5 is the latest version, and includes functionality which required other markup or scripting languages before. It offers several new, powerful tags which provide much stronger page structure. Cleaner and more readable code in the markup, along with greater structural capabilities, means better and more functional pages with HTML5.

Get the web browser(s)

Web browsers are familiar pieces of software, but not all web browsers are the same. Mainstream Internet browsers are all HTML5-compliant to varying extents, but a few are outstanding in their degree of compliance. Downloading a few browsers will make sure your HTML pages display the way you want them to in as many browsers as possible.

1 Identify the browser you use to view Internet pages.

2 Navigate to http://www.google.com/chrome.

3 Click the Download Google Chrome button to download the Chrome browser.

4 After downloading completes, open the download location and install the Google Chrome browser.

5 Download the Opera browser by navigating to http://opera.com and clicking the Browser link.

6 Download the Safari browser from http://support.apple.com/downloads/#safari.

> **Get Chrome, a fast new web browser.**
>
> **Download Google Chrome**
>
> For Windows 7/Vista/XP
> It's **free** and installs in minutes.

3

 ALERT: Google Chrome, like many other software programs now, requires an active Internet connection to download and install the software. Be sure your computer is online to get it.

? DID YOU KNOW?
Computers come with a web browser already installed. Windows computers use Internet Explorer, while many Linux computers have Mozilla Firefox and Apple computers have Safari. For the tasks in this book, make sure the browser is familiar and comfortable to use. Most screenshots in this book are of either Opera, Safari for Windows or Chrome.

HOT TIP: Your computer is probably set up to open HTML documents with the default web browser. Double-clicking on any file with the extension .html or .htm will open it in the browser specified as the default.

 ALERT: Be sure to download the correct version of the browser you choose from the selections available. If your computer uses Windows, download the Windows version of the browser; for Linux or Unix, choose those installation files. Installing the wrong version for your operating system can cause problems, not least of which is that the browser won't work!

Get the text editor(s)

Creating HTML pages doesn't require much equipment. All you need is a computer, an Internet web browser such as Internet Explorer or Mozilla Firefox, and a text editor like Notepad. Any web page imaginable can be created with just these few items. Gathering a text editor to mark up your documents is the first order of business.

1 Decide whether you'll use the text editor which came with your computer or a feature-enhanced one.

2 To download Notepad++, open a web browser to http://notepad-plus-plus.org/.

3 Click the download tab at the top of the screen.

notepad-plus-plus.org/release/5.9

free as in both "free speech" and "free beer"

Notepad++

3

Current Version: 5.9

DOWNLOAD   NEWS   ONLINE HELP   RESOURCES   CONTRIBUTIO

Notepad++ 5.9 Release

Release Date: 2011-03-31
- Notepad++ v5.9 Installer
- Notepad++ v5.9 zip package
- Notepad++ v5.9 7z package
- Notepad++ v5.9 minimalist package
- SHA-1 digests for binary packages
- Notepad++ v5.9 code source (source code)

*new 2 - Notepad++
File Edit Search View Encoding Language Settings Macro Ru
Window ?

new 2

This is Notepad++, installed and ready to go!

4 Click the Download current version link on the screen.

5 When prompted, save the file to an easy-to-remember location on your computer.

6 Browse to the file you just saved and double-click it to install Notepad++; use all default options.

> **! ALERT:** Don't confuse text editors with word processors or *rich* text editors! Modern word processors can create HTML documents, but generally add hidden codes which can cause browsers to display incorrectly. Rich text editors do not add as much code, but do add some. Text editors add no formatting or additional code, which is why they are used for HTML markup.

 DID YOU KNOW?
Most computers come with a text editor. But text editors with enhanced functionality can help create HTML documents. Notepad++, a cost-free text and code editing software, can be downloaded from http://notepad-plus-plus.org/.

? DID YOU KNOW?
HTML editors are designed to create HTML documents. Think of them as HTML word processors, with specific commands and formatting for HTML. HTML5-specific tags are not usually available in HTML editors.

Download an HTML quick reference guide

Having information at your fingertips makes any task easier. Working with HTML5 and CSS3 is no exception. To make sure you have a quick reference of the tags and properties you'll need to work with while doing web design, or as a reference for working the tasks in this book, the quick reference guides (or QRGs) in this task are invaluable.

1 Open your web browser.

2 Navigate to http://veign.com/.

3 Download the free Quick Reference Guide for HTML5. The specific web address is http://www.veign.com/reference/html5-guide.php.

4 Look over the other QRGs available on this page: http://www.veign.com/reference/index.php.

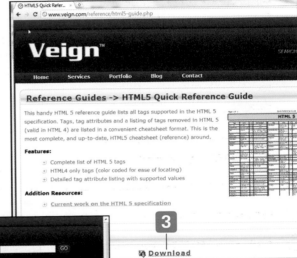

DID YOU KNOW?

It's always good practice to bookmark sites which provide reference and valuable information. Be sure to add Veign.com to your favourite websites!

HOT TIP: Save the files you create and download to places in your computer which are easy to remember and find. A reference guide you can't locate won't provide any help!

Download a CSS3 quick reference guide

HTML5 goes hand in hand with CSS3. CSS3 will be covered later in this book, but to prepare, QRGs are available on the Internet to download. They'll prove valuable when you're working through the tasks in this book, or when you're taking on a full web page design.

1 Open your web browser.

2 Navigate to Veign.com (http://veign.com/).

3 Download the free quick reference guide for CSS3 (located at http://www.veign. com/reference/css3-guide.php).

4 Feel free to look over all the reference guides at http://www. veign.com/reference/index.php.

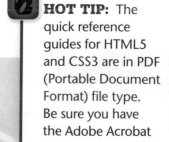

ALERT: Be sure to save the file in a location you will recall later!

HOT TIP: The quick reference guides for HTML5 and CSS3 are in PDF (Portable Document Format) file type. Be sure you have the Adobe Acrobat Reader or some PDF-capable equivalent to open and view them.

Understand HTML tags

HTML is a markup language made of tags, elements and attributes. *Tags* are angle brackets with a set of instructions for how the browser displays what is between the tags. HTML tags tell the browser what comes between them so the browser will properly display the content.

| Start tag | Content | End tag |

`<h1>This is a title element</h1>`

3 4

 1 Open your text editor.

2 Type an angle bracket (<). (This is also called the 'less-than' sign.)

3 Type the letter 'h' and the digit '1'.

4 Type another angle bracket (or 'greater-than' sign) (>).

HOT TIP: Copying and pasting in HTML scripting will save you a lot of time and typing. If a tag, an element or an attribute will be used many times, copy and paste it to the various locations in the document.

```
1 <h1>
```

? DID YOU KNOW?

HTML tags and elements are terms which have distinct meanings, but in common usage are interchangeable. Most web designers and developers do not distinguish between tags and elements any more. The terms are used interchangeably in this book as well.

Understand HTML elements

HTML *elements* are sets of tags with content between them, such as text or a picture. Things like headings, paragraphs and tables are elements. Most HTML elements have a *start tag* and an *end tag*. The start tag tells the browser how to display the content which follows it. The end tag tells the browser the element has ended and new instructions will follow.

1 Open your text editor.

2 Type an HTML heading 1 element (`<h1></h1>`).

3 Between the start and end tags, type the text 'This is a title element'.

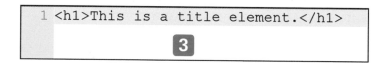

4 Save the file with the name testhtml.htm.

5 Open the newly saved file with your web browser to view the results.

? DID YOU KNOW?

You can use your browser to open documents which aren't on the Internet. Just go to the File menu and choose the Open menu selection. In the Open dialogue box, navigate to the file you want to open or view. In Google Chrome, use the Ctrl + O keystroke combination to launch the Open dialogue box.

? DID YOU KNOW?

There are two slash characters on most standard keyboards. The one which leans from top right to bottom left like this / is the forward slash. For most HTML purposes, this is the only slash you will need.

Understand HTML attributes

HTML *attributes* define how an element looks or behaves. The specific image to display, or the specific web page to link to, or the specific video to embed in a web page are all examples of attribute settings. Some HTML elements require attributes and others do not.

Many HTML tag attributes can be adjusted to alter the display. Attributes are only listed in start tags, and placed in single or double quotes to ensure compatibility with older HTML or XHTML versions:

```
<img src="http://somelinktoapicture.com/"></img>
```

The image tag `<img>` in the example above has a required attribute of `src` (or source), which specifies the location of the image to be displayed.

1. Open your text editor.

2. Type an HTML heading 1 element on the first line (`<h1></h1>`).

3. In the start tag, type a space after the h1, and then the following: style="color: red"

4. Type 'This is a title element' between the tags. (Do not include the quotes.)

5. Save the file with a new file name (remember to make it easy to recall!) and .htm or .html extension.

6. Open the newly saved file in your web browser to view the results.

? DID YOU KNOW?
HTML5 does not require single or double quotes around attribute values. Older markup languages do, however, so it is good practice to use them when marking up your HTML documents.

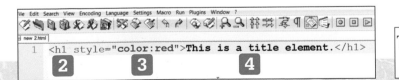

This is a title element.

WHAT DOES THIS MEAN?

Extension: a three- or four-character file type designator which follows the 'dot' in the file name. For example, .txt is a text file and designates an unformatted file of text only; .doc is a Microsoft Word document; etc.

Bookmark reference sites

While working with HTML5 and CSS3, you'll find it useful and convenient to bookmark some of the more informative or helpful sites you encounter. You'll probably refer to them often. Over time your favourite sites will become clear to you, but to help you get started here are a few terrific resources which should prove valuable.

1 Open your web browser to the World Wide Web Consortium's website, http://www.w3.org/.

2 Locate the bookmark utility for your browser.

3 Add the W3C site to your bookmarks.

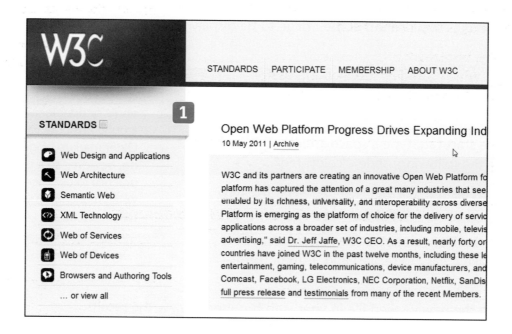

DID YOU KNOW?

The World Wide Web Consortium, or W3C, is an Internet standards world-wide governing body. It provides a way for Internet software and languages providers to agree on standards for Internet technologies. Companies such as Microsoft, Apple, IBM, Hewlett-Packard and others come together to agree on changes to Internet-specific languages and technologies, like HTML, CSS and web browsers. The W3C keeps compliance standards, recommended revisions and the current state of most web technologies.

ALERT: 'Bookmark' is the term most browsers use for saving favourite websites. Microsoft Internet Explorer uses the term 'Favorites' instead.

4 Now navigate to the w3schools website at http://w3schools.org/ and bookmark it as well.

5 Navigate to the Web Design Group's (WDG) site at http://htmlhelp.com/ and add it, too.

6 Bookmark http://veign.com/ (from which you downloaded the QRGs earlier).

7 Now browse to www.whatwg.org, home of the Web Hypertext Application Technology Working Group (WHATWG).

8 Finally, bookmark http://www.css3.info/, which contains succinct and useful information on the CSS3 specification.

 DID YOU KNOW?
Google Chrome doesn't have a bookmark button. Instead, click the star icon in the Omni box (the combination address bar and search engine entry bar) to bookmark a web page.

 **7**
Welcome to the WHATWG community
Maintaining and evolving HTML since 2004

 DID YOU KNOW?
The WHATWG works alongside the W3C on HTML specifications. There is a long and interesting story as to how the WHATWG became the standards working group for HTML5 rather than the W3C itself, which still maintains the standards as they are produced by the WHATWG. That story can be found by doing a simple Internet search.

Find 'Lorem ipsum' text

'Lorem ipsum' text is placeholder text used as filler on pages for typesetting and graphic design. It's also helpful for website design, however, and we will use it several times throughout the book to provide quick and easy text you can copy and paste into a web page. It will let you quickly create some lines, paragraphs or even whole pages of text so you can get to the fun part: the markup!

1 Navigate to http://www.lipsum.com/.

2 Add the site to your bookmarks.

3 Choose the language you want to use from the top of the page.

4 Select the number of paragraphs, words, bytes or lists to generate.

5 Tick or untick the 'Start with Lorem ipsum…' box.

6 Click the Generate Lorem Ipsum button.

 DID YOU KNOW?
You can search for 'Lorem ipsum generators' in your favourite Internet search engine to find other online tools to generate placeholder text.

> Lorem ipsum dolor sit amet, consectetur adipiscing elit. Nunc ac pellen fermentum, libero leo malesuada tellus, a scelerisque est mauris a felis. Al quam. In hac habitasse platea dictumst. Nulla faucibus egestas magna, ve eu est scelerisque tristique. Pellentesque porta metus a turpis viverra eu c commodo ullamcorper. Nam gravida consectetur imperdiet. Donec odio nu Phasellus non mauris purus, sed commodo lacus. Quisque eget velit se natoque penatibus et magnis dis parturient montes, nascetur ridiculus mu non ultricies tellus. Proin eu justo tellus, id aliquet lacus. Vestibulum an posuere cubilia Curae; Phasellus hendrerit malesuada nulla, quis aliquam

 HOT TIP: Copy and paste the generated 'Lorem ipsum' text to a text document using your text editor and save it with an easily recalled file name.

DID YOU KNOW?
Placeholder text used in printing and graphics design is commonly known as 'Lorem ipsum' text. There are several 'Lorem ipsum' text generators on the Internet you can use.

2 Structuring documents with HTML5

Introduction

As stated in Chapter 1, HTML is a set of instructions for the web browser. For example, the markup `<b>Text to display on screen</b>` tells the web browser to show the text between the `<b>` and `</b>` tags as bold face type.

In this chapter you'll use the basic tools you'll need – a browser and text editor – to create HTML elements. You'll gain an understanding of how those elements make up the HTML document structure. Later in the book, you'll learn how to format those elements individually to customise the look and feel of your web page.

Create a basic HTML document

All HTML documents have two primary sections: the header and the body. All the content of the page, everything you see and interact with, is in the body. The header contains data which is not visible, content the user or viewer doesn't actually see. Some elements common to HTML documents include the Document Type Declaration (DTD), the HTML (`<html></html>`) element, the head (`<head></head>`) element, and the body (`<body></body>`) element.

1 Open a new document in your text editor.

2 At the top of the document type `<!DOCTYPE html>`. This is the HTML Document Type Declaration.

3 In your text editor, on a new line type in the start and end tags for the HTML element, like this:
`<html></html>`

4 Create the start and end tags for the head element (`<head></head>`) between the HTML element tags.

5 Create the body element (`<body></body>`) inside the HTML element after the head element.

6 Save the file with a new name in an easy-to-remember location.

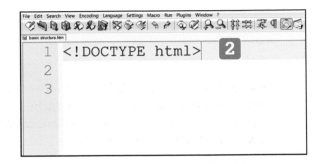

> **SEE ALSO:** The first line of a standards-compliant HTML document, regardless of whatever else is included, is the Document Type Declaration (also called the Doctype Declaration or DTD). With HTML5 the DTD is very simple. It is:
>
> `<!DOCTYPE html>`
>
> This DTD will work with earlier versions of HTML on web pages, too. The DTD tells the browser to expect an HTML document instead of another type of document. Because of the DTD's function, there must be no blank lines before it. If the browser encounters a blank line before the DTD, it will behave as though there is no DTD and the results may be unpredictable.

27

Create an HTML title

An HTML document title is the text you see in the title bar at the top of your web browser's window when you open a page. It lets a visitor to the page know where they are. You will place a title in the head section of an HTML file and view the document in your web browser to see the title in the title bar and on the tab, if your browser uses them (most do now).

1 Open the basic HTML file you created earlier in this chapter.

2 Save the file with a new name. Be sure to give it the .htm or .html file name extension.

3 Inside the head element (i.e. between the `<head>` and `</head>` tags), place the cursor and create a title element with a start and end tag (`<title></title>`).

4 Between the `<title>` and `</title>` tags, type some text such as 'My In Simple Steps Document'.

5 Save the document, then open it in your web browser to view the results.

> **SEE ALSO:** See the 'Create a basic HTML document' task earlier in this chapter for the file details.

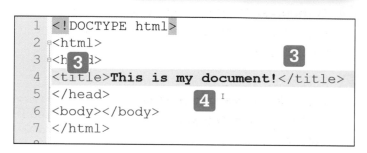

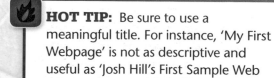

> **ALERT:** Be sure to make the new file name meaningful to you. For instance, 'task1.html' may not be as helpful as 'chapter1webpage.html' later on.

HOT TIP: Be sure to use a meaningful title. For instance, 'My First Webpage' is not as descriptive and useful as 'Josh Hill's First Sample Web Page'. I would use the latter as my title.

HOT TIP: You can save the basic file you created as an HTML template, which you can use for many of the subsequent tasks in this book.

Add content to the body element

The HTML body element (`<body></body>`) is where all the content of a web page resides. All the things you can see, interact with or hear are contained in the body element. The body element follows the head element on an HTML page, and is made up of both a start and an end tag.

1 Place the cursor between the `<body>` and `</body>` tags.

2 Type 'Hello, World!' in the body element, then save the HTML document with a new file name.

3 Open the HTML document in your web browser to see the content you added in the main part of the screen.

29

? DID YOU KNOW?
Notice the body element comes after the `</head>` tag; that is, it comes after the head element.

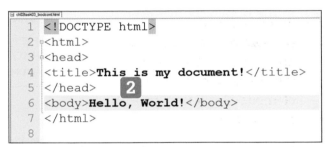

```
   ch02task03_bodcont.html
1  <!DOCTYPE html>
2  <html>
3  <head>
4  <title>This is my document!</title>
5  </head>        2
6  <body>Hello, World!</body>
7  </html>
8
```

Hello, World!

ALERT: Do not use the quote marks when you add content to the body element of your HTML page, or they will be displayed as part of the content itself. They are used in the examples in this book to show what you should type, but unless otherwise stated, should not be used.

HOT TIP: If you use a tabbed-interface browser (most of them are now), you will notice the title you put in the title element of your sample HTML document will also appear as the title of the tab on which the page opens.

Create HTML comments

Comments in HTML are not displayed on the screen. This makes comments useful for adding notations, or hiding things not meant to be seen. HTML comments have an opening angle bracket followed by an exclamation point. The exclamation point is then followed by two dashes (or hyphens). Any text, script data, or style code is added. The comment is followed by another pair of dashes and then the closing angle bracket:

```
<!-- This is an HTML comment -->
```

There is no limit to how many lines you can put in an HTML comment. This enables you to place a great deal of script, style or notation information in them.

1 Open the HTML document you made earlier in this chapter with your text editor.

2 In the body (`<body></body>`) element, create a few blank lines.

3 In the middle of the white space, type the opening comment marker `<!--`.

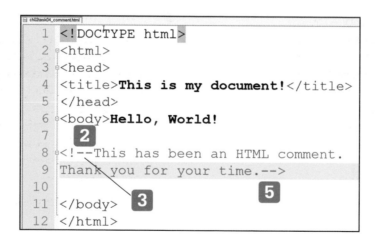

```
ch02task04_comment.html
 1  <!DOCTYPE html>
 2  <html>
 3  <head>
 4  <title>This is my document!</title>
 5  </head>
 6  <body>Hello, World!
 7      2
 8  <!--This has been an HTML comment.
 9  Thank you for your time.-->
10                              5
11  </body>     3
12  </html>
```

? DID YOU KNOW?

Many web pages include Cascading Style Sheet code in the heading of the HTML document to prevent it from showing in the display. Older browsers still recognise the head element as information not displayed, and therefore do not show it. Many scripts are also placed inside the head element, before the title element, of HTML documents.

 HOT TIP: This is a good opportunity to paste in some Lorem ipsum text from a generator to use as an HTML comment.

4 Type a few remarks, either one which is several lines long or a single sentence copied repeatedly.

5 After the comment text, type the closing comment marker -->.

6 Save the HTML document with a new name, and open it in your web browser.

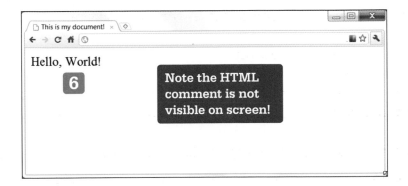

HOT TIP: Despite the similarity in appearance, the opening and closing for an HTML comment isn't called a 'tag'. But you can think of it as a tag, since both a start and end marker is required.

DID YOU KNOW?

Your comments are visible to any reader through the View Source function of their web browser. Many web developers and programmers use this information when working with web pages designed or programmed by others. Make sure you take advantage of the HTML comment feature.

Add HTML sections

The section element, which requires both a start and end tag like this, `<section>` `</section>`, creates a division or section in an HTML document. Sections can be grouped by content, theme or be part of an application or form. Sections generally have a header and sometimes a footer (those elements are covered later in more detail).

The `<section>` element can also be nested, which means a section can be subdivided into more sections using more `<section></section>` elements. Each section can also have its own header and footer.

1 Open your HTML document with your text editor and save it with a new file name.

2 In the body element, insert a section element, i.e. `<section></section>`.

3 Type 'This is an HTML section!' between the start and end tags.

4 Save the HTML file and open it using your browser to see the new content you've added.

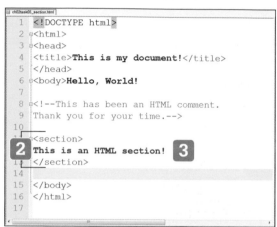

```
    1   <!DOCTYPE html>
    2   <html>
    3   <head>
    4   <title>This is my document!</title>
    5   </head>
    6   <body>Hello, World!
    7
    8   <!--This has been an HTML comment.
    9   Thank you for your time.-->
   10
        <section>
   2    This is an HTML section!   3
        </section>
   14
   15   </body>
   16   </html>
   17
```

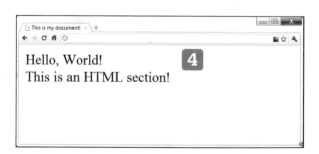

Hello, World!
This is an HTML section!   **4**

! ALERT: There are other grouping elements, such as the `<article>` element and the `<aside>` element, covered later in this chapter. Most of the elements grouped together will be grouped thematically. All articles will be grouped together; any asides or sidebars will be grouped together; and so on.

? DID YOU KNOW?

If you want to remove the 'Hello, World!' content to clean up your file, you can; it won't be needed any further.

🔥 HOT TIP: It is generally good practice to place the start and end tags of an element on different lines in an HTML file so content can be added and removed more easily.

Add HTML articles

The article element divides a page into discrete articles such as forum or blog posts. The article element requires a start and end tag. Article elements can be used to subdivide a section into magazine or newspaper style articles.

1 Using your text editor, open your HTML document and save it with a new name.

2 In the section element, add an article element, i.e. `<article></article>`.

3 In the start tag for the article element, add the following: `style="background: palegreen; display:block"`

4 Between the article element tags, add some text. You can use your Lorem ipsum generator if you like.

5 Save the HTML file and open it in your web browser.

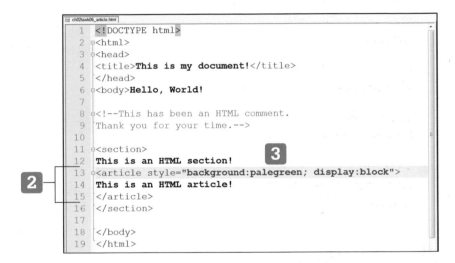

```
ch02task06_article.html
 1  <!DOCTYPE html>
 2  <html>
 3  <head>
 4  <title>This is my document!</title>
 5  </head>
 6  <body>Hello, World!
 7
 8  <!--This has been an HTML comment.
 9  Thank you for your time.-->
10
11  <section>
12  This is an HTML section!              3
13  <article style="background:palegreen; display:block">
14  This is an HTML article!
15  </article>
16  </section>
17
18  </body>
19  </html>
```

This is my document!

Hello, World!
This is an HTML section!
This is an HTML article!   **5**

Note the green background!

HOT TIP: The information you added to the start tag in step 3 is called an inline style, and is CSS, not HTML. CSS is covered in more detail later in the book. Because CSS is different from HTML, the quote marks are required, and in this instance must be included when you add the text.

 DID YOU KNOW?

Many elements of HTML5 aren't visible without using CSS to highlight them. CSS is covered in more detail later in the book.

Create HTML navigation

The nav element (`<nav></nav>`) provides an area for navigation and primary links. Before HTML5, other means had to be used to create navigational elements like menus and links in lists. The nav element creates a section for grouping site navigation links.

1 Open your HTML document and save it with a new name.

2 In the body element, before the section element, add a `<nav>` element (`<nav></nav>`).

3 On a separate line, type 'Link 1' (no quotes), then press the Enter key.

4 Type 'Link 2' and 'Link 3' (again, no quotes), each on its own line.

5 Save the HTML file and open it with your browser.

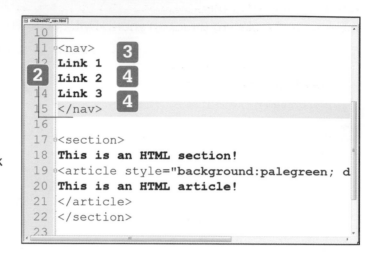

```
10
11  <nav>
12   Link 1
13   Link 2
14   Link 3
15  </nav>
16
17  <section>
18  This is an HTML section!
19  <article style="background:palegreen; d
20  This is an HTML article!
21  </article>
22  </section>
23
```

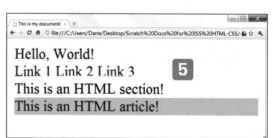

Hello, World!
Link 1 Link 2 Link 3
This is an HTML section!
This is an HTML article!

? DID YOU KNOW?

While the `<nav>` element is designed for use with site navigational links, other links and sidebar data can be placed in it as well. Like all other HTML elements, the contents are up to the site designer.

? DID YOU KNOW?

Even though you placed each link on a separate line, the browser displayed all the links on the same line. This is because we didn't issue any instructions for the browser to show them on different lines, and the web browser doesn't recognise the Enter key as a line break. HTML has several ways to do this and we'll cover them later in this book.

HOT TIP: Not all tags in HTML have start and end tags. All structural elements, however, do require both a start and end tag to mark where the structure starts and ends, and what it contains.

Create an HTML sidebar

The aside element has a start and end tag, and creates a sidebar section to a page. The aside element creates a grouping specifically for content sometimes related to the main content, or navigational aids, such as links to external sites. The name implies the aside often found in print media, but can also be a section where widgets and other links of interest can be placed, similar to a nav element.

1 Open your sample web page in your text editor and save it with a new name.

2 In the body tag, under the nav element, add the aside element (`<aside></aside>`).

3 Between the aside element tags, type 'This is the sidebar!' (without the quotes).

4 Add at least one paragraph of text in the aside element.

5 Save the HTML file and open it in your web browser.

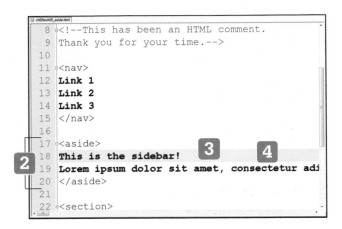

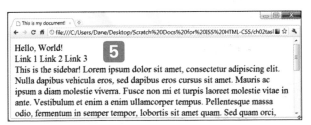

> **? DID YOU KNOW?**
> The sidebar can be formatted independently of other elements on the page with CSS. This is true for all structural elements in HTML5.

> **? DID YOU KNOW?**
> The web page content may seem a little muddled right now, but CSS formatting will help clear it up visually and make it appealing. HTML is suited to structures, not formatting, which has been moved to CSS3 for the most part.

> **! ALERT:** The aside and nav elements are similar, but in practice there are differences. Those examining the code should be able to understand the decisions the original designer made. So use the nav element for site navigation or links to other documents and keep the sidebar created with the aside element for tangentially related content, as a matter of good practice.

Create an HTML content header

Headers for sections, articles and even for aside and nav sections are created using the header (`<header></header>`) element. The header element defines a section of headings and subheadings. Header elements usually contain at least one heading element. But elements that section an HTML document don't go inside the header element, and the header element does not have to be inside an element which sections an HTML page, though it typically is.

There's nothing fancy to learn about headers. They're sections on an HTML page very much like the `<section>` and `<aside>` elements, for headings to things like articles, blog posts, etc. Like all structural HTML5 elements, they require a start and end tag and can have their own formatting applied.

1 In your text editor, open the HTML document you've created and save it with a new name.

2 In the body element, above the nav element, add the start and end tag for the header element (`<header></header>`).

3 In the start tag, add this inline style: `style="display:block"`

4 Between the tags type 'This is the page header!' (without the quotes).

5 Save the HTML file and open it in your web browser.

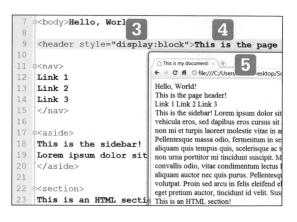

 HOT TIP: HTML has both a *header* element (`<header></header>`) and *heading* elements (designated by `<h1>` through to `<h6>` tags). The names look alike and aren't always easy to tell apart. But they are very different. A header is a section of an HTML document or web page; a heading is formatting applied to content such as text. Headings will be covered in a later chapter.

HOT TIP: The `style="display:block"` property places the element on its own line in your browser window. We're doing this for visual clarity. Experiment with it to make visual sense of your web page. CSS is covered in more detail later in the book.

Create an HTML footer

Most web pages have a dedicated footer section, which can contain anything, but generally is used for links to copyright information, navigation aids or pages on the site. HTML5 provides the footer (`<footer></footer>`) element for this purpose. It requires both a start and end tag, and any content between the tags displays in a footer section. The footer element can also be applied to a section, an article or for an entire website.

1 Open your HTML document in your text editor and save it with a new name.

2 In the body element, below all other elements and above the `</body>` tag, add an HTML footer element (`<footer></footer>`).

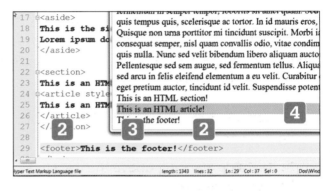

3 Between the footer tags, type 'This is the footer!'. (Remember, no quotes!)

4 Save the HTML document and open it in your web browser.

 HOT TIP: If you need to modify the footers to see them more clearly, add the same inline style to the start tags as you did in the last task.

 DID YOU KNOW?
An article footer can be used to link to a main site where the source material is located, a by-line for the journalist or writer, or links to related articles.

 DID YOU KNOW?
The footer is related to the element which contains it. It's a page footer if it's placed in the body element of a page. It's the section footer if it's placed before the end tag of a section element. If added to an article element it's the article footer, and so on.

 DID YOU KNOW?
The footer element can contain longer text as well as short informational bits of content. In the cases where an entire section is added in a footer element, it can be used as an appendix, or contain long text such as licence agreements. The footer adds a great deal of flexibility to web page structural design.

3 Using HTML text markup tags

Introduction

HTML groups and structures text into organised units like paragraphs and citations or blockquotes using simple tags and elements applied to text rather than to the page itself. In this chapter you'll experiment with basic HTML text structuring and formatting and apply it to text, and then view the results in a web browser.

You'll also learn how to create and customise one of the most basic and well-known features of HTML – the hyperlink. With a simple tag and its attributes and settings, hyperlinks can be created to link to parts of a page, to other pages on the same site, or to external sites.

Break text into paragraphs

The most basic grouping of text is the paragraph. With HTML, the paragraph can serve as a logical grouping of text, like in print, or to separate text from the surrounding content. Any text placed in a paragraph element (`<p></p>`) appears as a single paragraph regardless of line breaks created in the text editor. Like paragraphs in word processors, HTML paragraphs are not first-line indented and are left-aligned by default.

The paragraph element requires a start tag, but the end tag is optional. It is good practice, however, to enclose all paragraph text in the full element, `<p>...</p>`.

Not placing the end tag on a paragraph element forces the browser to try to figure out where the paragraph ends and the next paragraph begins. While using only the start tag is common practice, it's always safer to use the end tag as a matter of code habit and to ensure proper interpretation of markup.

Web browsers also handle text wrapping automatically, so if there is a specific place where the text must move to a new line, it's necessary to use the break tag (`<br>`). Web browsers see this in the same way Microsoft Word or OpenOffice Writer word-processing software sees the Enter key. Without the break tag, the text will wrap at browser-determined margins (unless CSS has been used to establish them, of course).

 DID YOU KNOW?

Paragraph elements can also be used to generate white space free from any content. This is achieved by using an 'empty paragraph' element. When using an empty paragraph to create white space, it's good practice to include a non-breaking space in the paragraph element. This is done with a special character. Special characters are discussed later in this book in detail, but a non-breaking space is inserted with the character command   – the ampersand, nbsp and the ending semi-colon are all part of the special character.

WHAT DOES THIS MEAN?

Line break: the end of a line of text, either by encountering the page margin or by manual insertion of a line break such as pressing the Enter key in word-processor software.

Left-aligned: text is aligned to the left margin of the page with a ragged (or unjustified) right margin.

1. Open the HTML document in your text editor, and save it with a new name.

2. Put the text 'This is an HTML section!' inside the start and end tags of a paragraph element (`<p></p>`).

3. In the section element, above the article element, add a paragraph (your 'Lorem ipsum' generator can help!).

4. Enclose your new paragraph in the paragraph element.

5. Save the HTML file and open it in the web browser.

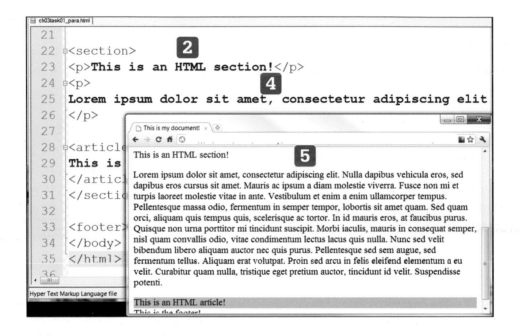

Add HTML headings

HTML has six different headings, shown as the heading element and level number. Think in terms of an outline. The top-most heading levels are <h1> elements. <h2> elements are subheadings, subdivided by <h3> sub-subheadings, etc. Higher-level headings are new sections, and lower headings subdivide the current level. Headings organise the page into topics and subjects clearly for the reader.

1 Open your HTML document and save with a new name.

2 In the section element, replace the <p> element with an <h1> element around 'This is an HTML section!'.

3 Add an <h2> element below the newly created <h1> element.

4 Add the text 'This is an HTML subheading!' between the <h2> and </h2> tags.

5 Save the HTML file and open it with the web browser.

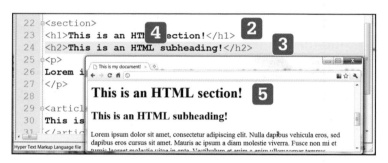

? DID YOU KNOW?

Heading elements format text. The text is generally changed in size and weight, and is offset from other content with white space. Heading elements require both a start and end tag. If you don't use an end tag, all of the text which follows the start tag will be interpreted by the browser as part of the heading level, and will be modified for display accordingly.

? DID YOU KNOW?

Some browsers allow you to view web pages in various styles. For instance, in Opera, from the View menu, you can choose Style, Outline and the page will display in outline format showing how content is grouped. Heading levels will be especially useful in these settings.

 HOT TIP: Use the Search and Replace feature of your text editor to locate text, tags and properties in your HTML document quickly and easily.

 HOT TIP: The formatting applied to each heading level is easily manipulated using CSS, which will be covered later in the book.

Group HTML headings

Headings can be grouped together using the `<hgroup>` element. This allows you to 'flatten' the outline so that a title and its subtitle, or a heading and its subheading, are viewed only at the top level in outline format. This works only in outline or summary views of the document, however, and the hgroup element does not have any visual impact on the web page.

1 Open your HTML document and save with a new name.

2 Add an `<hgroup>` tag before the `<h1>` tag in the section element.

3 Add the `</hgroup>` end tag after the `</h2>` tag in the section element.

4 Save the HTML document and open it in your web browser.

5 In the View Page Source option of your browser, locate the `<hgroup>` `</hgroup>` element.

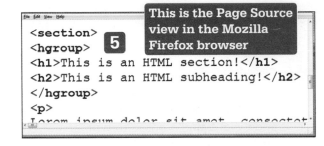

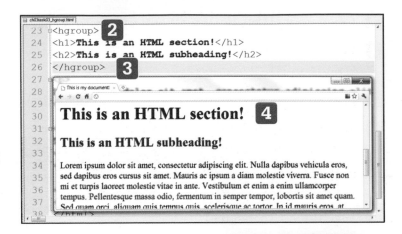

This is the Page Source view in the Mozilla Firefox browser

```
<section>
<hgroup>
<h1>This is an HTML section!</h1>
<h2>This is an HTML subheading!</h2>
</hgroup>
<p>
```

? DID YOU KNOW?
To have any effect, there must be more than one heading element inside the hgroup element.

! ALERT: The hgroup element requires a start and end tag, `<hgroup>...</hgroup>`.

! ALERT: Notice the `<hgroup>` element has no visual impact on the web page! A casual viewer will not notice its presence at all.

Emphasise text with HTML

To format text, HTML provides many elements which are added *inline* – that is, the content can be formatted in place and isn't separated from other content with white space. Examples are the italics (`<i></i>`) element, and more recently, the emphasis element (`<em></em>`). These add content formatting to anything between the start and end tags and provide a way to distinguish certain text elements from the rest.

1 Open your HTML document and save it with a new name.

2 Put the emphasis element (`<em></em>`) around the words 'Lorem ipsum dolor sit amet' in the paragraph in the aside (`<aside></aside>`) element.

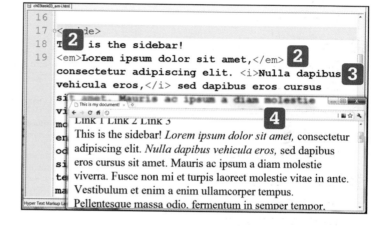

3 Enclose the first four words of the second paragraph in the italic (`<i></i>`) element.

4 Save the file and open it in your web browser.

? DID YOU KNOW?

Before CSS became the formatting method of choice, HTML provided basic ways to adjust text appearance on the screen. Some have survived into HTML5, while others are no longer supported by modern browsers.

? DID YOU KNOW?

It may be impossible to distinguish between certain formatting elements when applied to content, but HTML makes the distinctions among them for a reason. Using formatting elements such as italics (`<i></i>`) applies formatting directly to the text. The emphasis (`<em></em>`) element allows the browser to decide how to display emphasised content. It's a subtle but significant difference.

! ALERT: If you haven't used the 'Lorem ipsum' text generator to generate a paragraph in your aside element, use any part of a sentence in your HTML document that you like.

! ALERT: Like all inline formatting elements, the `<em>` and `<i>` elements require both a start and end tag. Leaving off the end tag causes *all* text after the start tag to be emphasis-formatted.

Format strong emphasis and bold text

Formatting text in a bold face is similar to formatting italics with HTML. There is an explicit element for making text bold (<b></b>), but the preferred way to format bold-face text, outside of CSS formatting, is to use the strong element (<strong></strong>). Using the strong element allows the browser's programming to decide how to strongly emphasise text, rather than simply making it bold.

1 Locate the paragraph in the section element on your HTML document in your text editor.

2 Place a strong element (<strong></strong>) around the first four or five words of the first sentence.

3 Find the first four or five words of the next sentence and enclose them in the bold (<b></b>) element.

4 Save the HTML document with a new name and open it in your web browser.

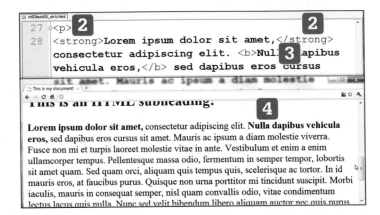

```
27  <p> 2
28  <strong>Lorem ipsum dolor sit amet,</strong>
    consectetur adipiscing elit. <b>Nul  3  apibus
    vehicula eros,</b> sed dapibus eros cursus
```

Lorem ipsum dolor sit amet, consectetur adipiscing elit. **Nulla dapibus vehicula eros,** sed dapibus eros cursus sit amet. Mauris ac ipsum a diam molestie viverra. Fusce non mi et turpis laoreet molestie vitae in ante. Vestibulum et enim a enim ullamcorper tempus. Pellentesque massa odio, fermentum in semper tempor, lobortis sit amet quam. Sed quam orci, aliquam quis tempus quis, scelerisque ac tortor. In id mauris eros, at faucibus purus. Quisque non urna porttitor mi tincidunt suscipit. Morbi iaculis, mauris in consequat semper, nisl quam convallis odio, vitae condimentum lectus lacus quis nulla. Nunc sed velit bibendum libero aliquam auctor nec quis purus

ALERT: Don't be alarmed if you can't tell the difference between text in the <b> element and text in the <strong> element. Most browsers currently handle them the same way.

? DID YOU KNOW?
Most of the job of making text look good on a web page has moved to Cascading Style Sheets, which does a better job of formatting and adjusting text appearance on a page. HTML still allows text formatting with a few elements, however, and they are easy to remember and use.

HOT TIP: You can leave the basic HTML document you're working with open in your text editor and simply use the Save As function (usually under the File menu) to save it with a new name from task to task to protect previous versions.

Format strikethrough and inserted text

HTML `<strikeout>` and `<u>` elements for strikethrough and underline text formatting, respectively, have been replaced by the insert and delete elements. The insert element (`<ins></ins>`) allows text to be emphasised as inserted or added to the content. The delete element (`<del></del>`) shows text as removed or struck through from the content. Many browsers display these tags as either strikeout (`<del>`) or underlined (`<ins>`) text, but browser manufacturers can display them in other ways as they choose.

1 Find the words 'Hello, World!' in the body element of your HTML document in your text editor.

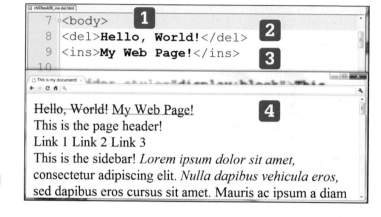

2 Enclose them with a delete (`<del></del>`) element.

3 Type the words 'My Web Page!' on the next line and enclose them in an insert (`<ins></ins>`) element.

4 Save the HTML document with a new name and open it in your browser.

HOT TIP: Use the Search or Find feature on your browser to locate the tags as you look for them if the browser allows it. This will make finding the various elements much faster.

? DID YOU KNOW?
While most browsers render the modern text formatting tags identically, the future may hold new ways of showing the various elements for emphasis, striking and insertion. CSS allows better control over how text is displayed, which is why it's the preferred method of formatting web page text.

! ALERT: Remember, browsers may show the same tags differently when using the `<ins>` and `<del>` tags! Most will show `<del>` and strikethrough (lined-through), but the `<ins>` tag may be rendered differently in Microsoft, Opera, Mozilla, Apple and Google browsers.

Use the \<small>, \<sup> and \<sub> elements

HTML has specific elements to create super- (\[\]) and subscript (_\) text. In addition, the small element (\<small>\</small>) reduces text size relative to surrounding text. Use the \<sup> element to reduce text and raise it above the baseline. Use the \<sub> script to reduce text size and move it below the baseline. Use the \<small> text to reduce text size and leave it on the baseline.

1 Open your HTML document in your text editor and save it with a new name.

2 Find the footer element and place the superscript element (\[\]) around the word 'This' inside it.

3 Place a small element (\<small>\</small>) around the words 'is the'.

4 Place a subscript (_\) element around the word 'footer'.

5 Save the file and open it in your web browser.

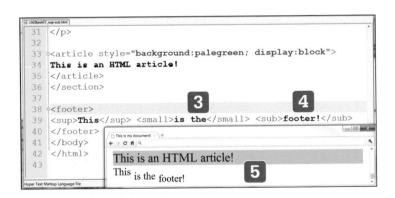

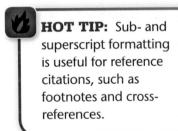

HOT TIP: Sub- and superscript formatting is useful for reference citations, such as footnotes and cross-references.

WHAT DOES THIS MEAN?

Superscript: text which is superscript to other text, i.e. it is elevated slightly above the line of text and reduced in size. Superscript text is often used for footnote indicator marks.

Subscript: text which is subscript to other text, i.e. it is lowered slightly beneath the line of text and reduced in size.

Format text as computer code

HTML provides a way to use monospaced fonts to represent computer code (`<code></code>`) or computer output samples (`<samp></samp>`). There is also markup for indicating a variable or a parameter for a specific application (`<var></var>`). You might use this when marking up examples of computer code or output, or to indicate where variables exist in technically oriented pages or resources.

1 Open your HTML document in your text editor and save it with a new name.

2 Locate the article element (`<article></article>`).

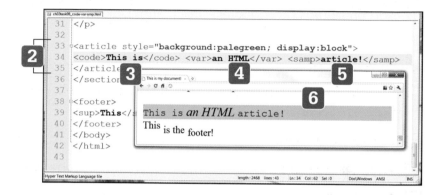

3 Enclose the words 'This is' in the code (`<code></code>`) element.

4 Wrap the words 'an HTML' in the `<var></var>` element.

5 Use a `<samp></samp>` element to enclose the word 'article!'.

6 Save the file and open it in your web browser.

? DID YOU KNOW?
Monospaced fonts are generally wider than variable-spaced fonts for the same font size. Changing a variable-width font to a monospaced font will change where the line breaks occur on screen.

! ALERT: Remember, some tags in HTML leave the display of the markup to the browser rather than specifying exactly how content should be formatted. If you don't see any differences in the markup elements on screen, it doesn't mean there won't be differences in the future.

WHAT DOES THIS MEAN?
Monospaced font: a font which uses the same letter spacing for all characters, rather than varying the spacing for each individual character. Courier and Courier New are well-known monospaced fonts.

Create manual line breaks

HTML allows manual line breaks using the break tag (<br>). The break tag is an open tag, meaning it has no end tag. It's made up of just the single tag. Use break tags to manually wrap text to a new line or create additional white space.

1 Open your HTML document with your text editor and find the <nav> element.

2 Add break tags (<br>) after 'Link 1' and 'Link 2'.

3 Locate the aside (<aside>) element.

4 After the text 'This is the sidebar!', insert a break tag (<br>).

5 Save the document and open it with your web browser.

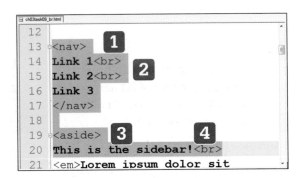

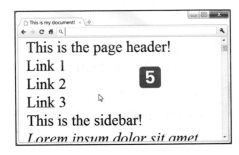

? **DID YOU KNOW?**

Earlier versions of HTML required a 'trailing slash' to be used on open tags, like this: <br />. HTML5, however, doesn't require a trailing slash, and in fact it may create unexpected behaviour in browsers encountering it. Many tutorials online are written for older versions of HTML and show the use of the trailing slash as part of open tag structure.

? **DID YOU KNOW?**

Creating white space in HTML documents can be done using block formatting tags like heading tags (<h1> through to <h6>), or with the paragraph tag (<p></p>), which inserts a blank line to move the content down two lines. The break tag (<br>) moves content down a single line without inserting a blank line in the content.

Create ordered lists

HTML lists provide bite-sized portions of numbered text. Numbered lists are called *ordered lists*, and require a start and end tag to create the list (`<ol></ol>`), and list item elements (`<li></li>`) to create individual list items.

1 Open your HTML document in your text editor and save it with a new name.

2 Find the navigation `<nav>` element and remove any break tags so the text is all on one line.

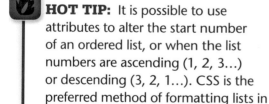

```
<nav>
<ol>
<li>Link 1</li>
<li>Link 2</li>
<li>Link 3</li>
</ol>
</nav>
```

1. Link 1
2. Link 2
3. Link 3

3 Wrap the 'Link' text contents in an ordered list element (`<ol></ol>`).

4 Wrap each of the three 'Link' items with a list item element (`<li></li>`).

5 Save the HTML file and open it in your web browser.

? DID YOU KNOW?
Ordered lists are typically used where the order of list items is important. Once specified by the ordered list element (`<ol></ol>`), ordered lists automatically number their list items sequentially from top to bottom, or from left to right if they're not separated by a line break in the HTML file. In the browser, they always display from top to bottom with numbers ascending in value.

HOT TIP: It is possible to use attributes to alter the start number of an ordered list, or when the list numbers are ascending (1, 2, 3…) or descending (3, 2, 1…). CSS is the preferred method of formatting lists in other ways, however.

 ALERT: Be sure to keep your ordered list element tags *inside* the `<nav>` element!

 ALERT: Remember to keep all list item elements (`<li></li>`) *inside* the ordered list element (`<ol></ol>`). This is *critical* for the list to display properly.

Create unordered lists

Unordered lists create orderly, organised lists without numbering. They're similar to ordered lists, but are used when the order of list items isn't important. They require a start and end tag for the list (`<ul></ul`) and contain at least one list item element (`<li></li>`).

1 Open your HTML document in your text editor and save it with a new name.

2 In the `<aside>` element, replace all `<ol>` tags with unordered list element tags (`<ul></ul>`).

3 Leave the list item elements (`<li></li>`) unchanged.

4 Save the HTML file and open it in your web browser.

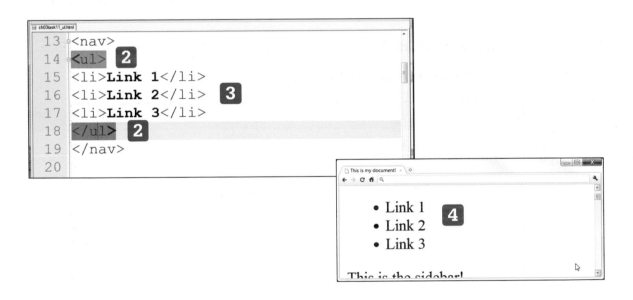

? DID YOU KNOW?

Unordered lists can be used to great effect in conjunction with other structural elements, like aside, section or footer elements, to create site maps and multi-level navigational aids for a website.

? DID YOU KNOW?

The list item element does not require an end tag if it's followed by another list item element, or if there's no other content in the parent element. It also allows nesting items to create an outline-style list.

Create description lists

Description lists are created with the description list element (`<dl></dl>`) and are useful for glossaries, defining terms and things like frequently asked questions (FAQ) pages. Description lists need at least one term to describe, and any number of descriptions or definitions. The list requires a start and end tag, and must contain at least one definition term element (`<dt></dt>`) and at least one description element (`<dd></dd>`).

1 Open your sample web page in the text editor and save it with a new name.

2 Find the `<nav>` element.

3 Replace the `<ul>` tags in the `<nav>` element with the definition list element (`<dl></dl>`).

4 Replace the list item element from around the 'Link 1' text with a definition term element (`<dt></dt>`).

5 Enclose the 'Link 2' and 'Link 3' text in definition description elements (`<dd></dd>`).

6 Save the HTML file and open it in your browser.

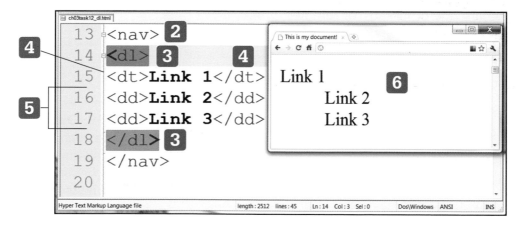

? DID YOU KNOW?

For the `<dt>` and `<dd>` elements an end tag is optional. Just as with every other optional end tag element, it is recommended you use the end tag to ensure proper interpretation of the element by the browser.

🔥 HOT TIP: The terms 'definition', 'name' and 'description' are all applied to the term to be described or defined in a description list, specified by the `<dt>` element. They are interchangeable so long as you remember not to confuse them with the descriptions and definitions signified by the `<dd>` element.

Use HTML quotations

HTML has a few ways to quote outside content. The quote element (`<q></q>`) specifies a short quotation, perhaps a sentence or two, and is usually used with the `cite` attribute to specify the source address. The blockquote element (`<blockquote></blockquote>`) specifies a longer quotation, set apart from the rest of the content due to its length or importance. It also uses the cite attribute to link to the quoted source's address. Finally, the cite element (`<cite></cite>`) refers to speakers in a conversation or individuals when quoting them.

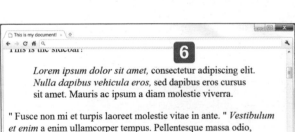

1 Open your HTML document in your text editor and save it with a new name.

2 Copy a 'Lorem ipsum' paragraph into the sidebar element, if you haven't done so already.

3 Enclose the first three sentences in a blockquote element (`<blockquote></blockquote>`). Disregard any other tags, or remove them if you'd like.

4 Enclose the fourth sentence in a quotation element (`<q></q>`).

5 Enclose the first three words of the next sentence in a citation (`<cite></cite>`) element.

6 Save the HTML file and open it in your web browser.

? DID YOU KNOW?

Blockquotes can also be used to call attention to specific content to entice readers, and separates the quote from the rest of the content with white space.

HOT TIP: Don't confuse the `cite` *attribute* of a quotation element with the cite *element*. The `cite` attribute is used within HTML quotation elements to link to the address of a quoted source. The cite element is used to format content as a citation.

WHAT DOES THIS MEAN?

Attribute: a specific property of an HTML element which alters how it is displayed or how it behaves. HTML element attributes are included in the start tag of the element.

4 Working with hyperlinks and images

Introduction

Hyperlinks let your browser fetch another page, a new site or multimedia, and bring it to your screen. Your browser only sees text, and hyperlinks send the browser to the correct resource to display. Hyperlinks can be text on screen or graphics.

Graphics make a web page unique. For the most part, there are three graphics formats. JPEG is the standard for images with many colour variations and is the best Internet-native format for photographs. JPEGs have the file extension .jpg or .jpeg. GIF was a standard for static, non-photo images and line art once, but has largely fallen out of use. It's still the native format for animated GIF images and uses the .gif extension. PNG is the standard for Internet artwork, has fantastic colour and file size properties, and allows advanced features like transparency. It uses the extension .png.

Use absolute URLs

Absolute URLs link sections of the same page, or pages on the same site, but are best suited to link to different sites, where the entire URL is required.

Absolute URLs use the anchor tag (`<a></a>`). A link location is specified in the href (or 'hyperlink reference') attribute. href is followed by an equal sign, double quotes (") and the full URL, including protocol and domain name. To link to a specific resource on the destination, the resource must be named.

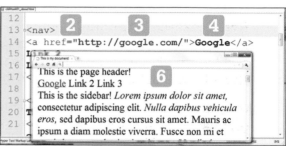

1. Open your HTML document in your text editor and save it with a new name.

2. Find the nav element (`<nav></nav>`).

3. Add a hyperlink to a favourite search engine by placing an anchor element (`<a href="http://url/path/resource">anchor text</a>`) around the 'Link 1' text.

4. Change the 'Link 1' text to the name of the website you linked to, such as Yahoo! or Google.

HOT TIP: A resource can be anything – a web page, a video clip, an audio file, an image or graphic, whatever. 'Resource' refers generically to anything the web browser can show you.

5. Repeat this process for all the list items in the aside element. Make sure you include the double quotes and the full path to the resource you're connecting to, if it's not the site's main page.

6. Save the HTML file and open it in your web browser. Click each hyperlink and make sure it takes you to the page or resource you hyperlinked to.

? DID YOU KNOW?
Internet addresses are called Uniform Resource Locators, or URLs. Every web page in the world, any resource on the web whether it's pure text or a mixture of text and multimedia or graphics, has its own specific URL. And URLs are the key to hyperlinks.

HOT TIP: The anchor text shown in step 3, except for the URL and path, is the exact format you should use when creating the hyperlinks for this task. If you like you can copy and paste the anchor tag from one list item element to the next and change the URLs as necessary.

Site navigation with relative URLs

Relative URLs are ideal for hyperlinking different pages of the same site. Relative URLs require only the directory name and path to the section or page to create a hyperlink. They tell the browser where on the same server to look using the href attribute of the anchor element (<a></a>), and the browser does the rest.

1 Open your HTML document with your text editor and save it with the name 'Main. htm'.

2 Go to File, Save As in your text editor and save it again with the name 'Sub1.htm'.

3 In Sub1.htm, remove all the elements inside the body element.

4 In the body element, add an <h1> element with the text 'This is Sub1' in it.

5 Enclose the <h1> element in an anchor element with an href attribute set to 'Main.htm'.

6 Save Sub1.htm and open 'Main.htm' in your text editor.

7 Remove all the elements inside the body element.

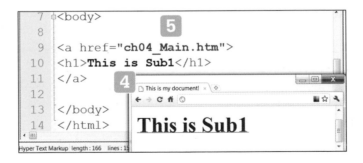

? DID YOU KNOW?

Domain names (or server names) of a web server are never case sensitive, but sometimes the path to a specific page or resource is. It depends on the server's operating system. Windows systems aren't case sensitive, but Unix servers are.

8 Add an <h1> element in the body element with the text 'This is Main'.

9 Enclose the <h1> element in an anchor element with an href attribute set to 'Sub1.htm'.

10 Save Main.htm and open it in your web browser.

11 Click the hyperlink to test it.

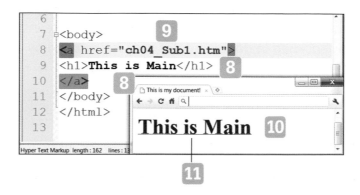

 ALERT: Every full stop, slash and quote mark is an essential part of a hyperlink. It won't work if they're not entered correctly.

 HOT TIP: Use the command `cd..` (that is, the letters 'cd' for 'change directory' and then two full stops) in relative URLs to navigate up in the directory structure. Use the command `cd./` (that is, the letters 'cd' for 'change directory', then a full stop, and then a forward slash) to navigate down in the directory structure. If the page is in the same folder, just list the file name.

Page navigation with hyperlink anchors

Connecting different parts of the same document is done via the anchor element and its href attribute. Hyperlinks connecting sections of the same page need to reference the sections they link to by name. To create the hyperlink, the anchor tag's href attribute points to another anchor with a name attribute instead of an href attribute. The name is enclosed in double quotes, and is preceded by a hash symbol (href="#destination").

1. Open the HTML document from an earlier task (don't use Main.htm or Sub1.htm), and save it with a new name.

2. Remove all tags and attributes from the `<nav>` element, and restore the text to 'Link 1', 'Link 2', etc.

3. Place an anchor element around the first link in the list with an href attribute set to "footer".

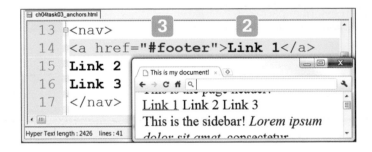

DID YOU KNOW?
Anchors can also link to other anchors on different pages. In this way, a link from one page can go not just to another page, but to a specific section of another page.

4 Locate the footer element and insert an anchor element with the name attribute set to "footer" inside the footer element.

5 Save the file and open it in your web browser. Click the `<nav>` element link to move to the footer.

? DID YOU KNOW?

When clicked, a hyperlink places the screen at the anchor location specified in the name attribute. The name attribute on the destination anchor does not require the hash symbol: `<a name="anchor name">`Destination Text`</a>`

WHAT DOES THIS MEAN?

Anchor: a special hyperlink which contains an href element that specifies another section of the same document.

Use hyperlink targets

The target attribute specifies where a browser opens a resource. The settings, each an underscore (_) followed by the target, are: _blank, _parent, _top, _self

_blank opens the resource in a new window or tab. _parent opens the parent window or tab, or the current one if there's no parent. _top opens the top-most window or tab, or the current one if it's the top level. _self opens in the current window or tab.

1. Open your HTML document and save it with a new name.

2. Locate the `<nav>` element and in the anchor element of the link, add the attribute `target="_blank"`.

3. In the second list item, add the attribute `target="_top"` to the anchor element.

4. In the third list item, add the attribute `target="_parent"` to the anchor element.

5. In the fourth list item, add the attribute `target="_self"` to the anchor element.

6. Save the HTML file and open it in your web browser. Test each link and observe the behaviour of the hyperlinks and where they open their destinations.

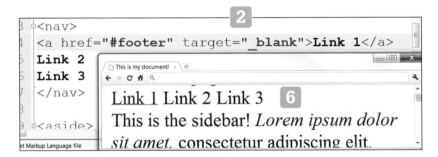

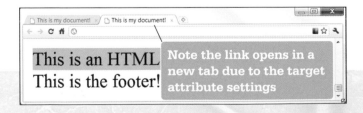

Note the link opens in a new tab due to the target attribute settings

? DID YOU KNOW?

The target attribute setting you'll use most frequently is _blank. As a web designer, the goal is to retain and attract visitors, not send them away.

Hyperlink to an email address

Many sites have a 'Contact' link which launches a form to send an email message. Rather than using the http protocol, hyperlinks to email addresses use the mailto protocol. In the href attribute, the mailto protocol and email address are provided and the hyperlink opens an email message to send to the address provided.

It's also possible to populate message fields, such as cc and bcc recipients and the subject line. In fact, you can even populate the body of the message if you want to. It becomes very cumbersome to quickly populate long messages, though.

Add a subject to the message by placing a question mark at the end of the email address, followed by 'subject', an equal sign (=) and then typing the subject line. Use &20 for spaces between words. To insert a cc recipient to the message, add &cc (ampersand cc) to the attribute, then an equal sign followed by the additional email address. Do the same to add a bcc recipient (replacing the cc with bcc, of course). Put body text in using &body then an equal sign and then the body of the message, again with &20 for spaces between words.

```
<a href="mailto:recipient1@webemail.com?
subject=Email&20Subject&20
&cc=recipient2@webemail.com
&bcc=recipient3@webemail.com
&body=I&20am&20contacing&20you.">Contact us!</a>
```

The enormous amount of typing makes populating more than the subject of the message and very short message bodies impractical.

 HOT TIP: Note that the entire href attribute value is wrapped in double quotes, but none of the individual values with it is wrapped in either single or double quotes. Doing so will cause the href value to be invalid and the hyperlink will not work.

 DID YOU KNOW?
Additional email addresses are added by separating them with semi-colons. There isn't a limit to how many addresses you can add to each field.

1. Open your HTML document with your text editor and save it with a new name.

2. Locate the nav element and find the 'Link 2' text, and enclose it in an anchor element.

3. Set the href element to the mailto protocol and your email address (`<a href="mailto:myemail@emailsvc.com">`).

4. Add a question mark *inside* the double quote *after* your email address.

5. Type the words 'subject='Email Hyperlink' after the question mark inside the quotes.

6. Save the HTML file and open it in a web browser and click the hyperlink to launch the message.

ALERT: If the subject line of your email doesn't display correctly, remove the space indicator characters &20 from between the subject line words in your HTML document, save the file and reload it in your web browser to try again.

Add images to a web page

Regardless of what shows on screen, an HTML file is only text. To show images, HTML uses the `<img>`, or image, tag. The browser needs the image location as a valid URL, given in the src attribute of the `<img>` tag, and it displays the image wherever the `<img>` tag is placed in the HTML file.

1. Open your HTML document in your text editor and save it with a new name.

2. Pick any open area in the `<body>` element of the page and add an image tag (`<img>`).

3. Set the src attribute in the image tag to the image's URL (use relative URLs for images on your computer or absolute URLs for images on the web).

4. Save the HTML file and open it with your web browser to observe the results.

? DID YOU KNOW?

The `<img>` tag isn't an element but a standalone tag. There is no end tag; instead a 'trailing slash' is used at the end of the start tag.

? DID YOU KNOW?

The pictures added to the web page are not positioned by the location of the `<img>` tag alone; CSS can be used to wrap text around the image, to place the image more precisely on the page, and to align the image horizontally and vertically with surrounding content.

Create image links

It's possible to create a hyperlink from an image rather than text. Instead of surrounding text with an anchor element (`<a></a>`), surround an image with one.

Some browsers place a blue border around the image when you create an image hyperlink. The border is to notify the user of the hyperlink.

 Open the HTML document with the image tag on it in your text editor and save it with a new name.

 Around the `<img>` tag, create an anchor element. Set the href attribute to open a favourite web page.

3 Set the target attribute to `_blank` to open it in a new tab or window.

4 Save the file and open it in your web browser, then click the image link to launch the web page.

HOT TIP: Not all browsers put the border around an image link, and the border colour depends on your personal browser settings.

SEE ALSO: See the 'Use absolute URLs' and 'Use hyperlink targets' sections for refreshers on setting href and target attributes for an anchor element.

? DID YOU KNOW?

If the image you chose is large (the one I used is *huge*), you can change the size with photo-editing software. Two very good (and free) image-editing software packages are GIMP (the Gnu Image Manipulation Program) and Paint.net (Windows-specific). An Internet search for free image-editing software will find many alternatives.

Create thumbnail image links

Image links are usually thumbnails. When the thumbnail is clicked, the browser loads the destination. Thumbnail size is set with the `<img>` tag height and width attributes, which change the thumbnail's display size. They're set in pixels and must be kept in the same aspect ratio, or the picture distorts.

1. Open the HTML file with the image link in your text editor and save it with a new name.

2. In the `<img>` tag, add the height and width attributes and set their values to 50.

3. Save the HTML file and open it in your web browser.

4. Click the thumbnail image to test the hyperlink.

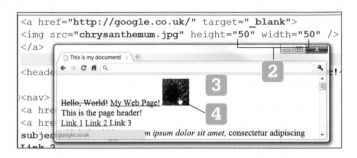

? DID YOU KNOW?

When using Google to search for images, when you click a thumbnail image, a frameset will load in the browser; the image will be in the bottom one, and the top will be the Google thumbnail.

HOT TIP: Remember, HTML tag attributes are input with the attribute name, an equal sign, then the value in double quotes, like this: `height="50" width="50"`

ALERT: Expect the thumbnail image to be distorted unless you use an image of equal height and width, because the aspect ratio probably will have been changed.

WHAT DOES THIS MEAN?

Aspect ratio: the ratio of width to height for a visual element, such as a video or image.

Mark up an image as a figure

To include an image on a web page as a figure linked to text content, such as where text refers to a specific image or graphic, simply encapsulate the image tag with the `<figure>` element. To include a caption, add a `<figcaption>` element with the text content to designate as the caption, inside the `<figure>` element.

A high-resolution image can be huge, both in file size and in physical dimensions. When dealing with Internet pages, designing for screen resolutions lower than 1024 by 768 pixels isn't necessary, but to see the image on the screen without using scroll bars or reducing the browser's zoom view, avoid using large files or include a thumbnail of the full image for users to click to see the full-sized image.

1 Open your HTML document in your text editor and save it with a new name.

2 Locate the image tag and enclose it in a `<figure>` element.

3 Before the `</figure>` tag, add a `<figcaption>` element with the content 'Figure 1' between the tags.

4 Save the HTML file and open it in your browser to view the results.

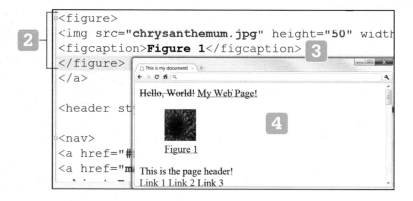

? DID YOU KNOW?

You can also use multiple images for a single figure. All images used are enclosed in the `<figure>` element. The `<figcaption>` element, if used, must either come before any figure content, or after all figure content. Each `<figure>` element can have only one `<figcaption>`.

? DID YOU KNOW?

Different browsers render images differently; some show figure captions to the lower right of the image, others render a blue border around the image and place the caption directly beneath the figure, etc.

5 Working with HTML tables

Introduction

Tables are columns and rows of cells to house data or content such as images, multimedia content, Internet pages from the same site or hyperlinks to other sites, and more.

HTML tables can also be used for page layout. Sectioning with tables makes the layout easy and much more efficient, not to mention more attractive, than using framesets.

HTML tables are built with row and cell elements. Cells can span both rows and columns to create larger divisions within the table. Borders, cell padding and cell spacing (covered in more detail later) can be handled using the `<table>` element's attributes or with CSS.

Create an HTML table structure

An HTML table is made of many nested elements rather than a single element. The first is the `<table></table>` element, which designates where the table resides. The browser is aware that the following elements and tags are all part of the table.

1 Open the HTML document with your text editor and save it with a new name.

2 In the body element, add a table (`<table></table>`) element.

3 In the start tag add the following to set the border width to one pixel: border="1"

4 Save the HTML file and open it in your web browser.

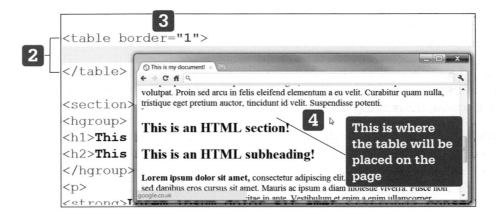

```
                            3
                    <table border="1">
   2

                    </table>

                    <section>
                    <hgroup>
                    <h1>This
                    <h2>This
                    </hgroup>
                    <p>
                    <strong>T
```

This is my document!

volutpat. Proin sed arcu in felis eleifend elementum a eu velit. Curabitur quam nulla, tristique eget pretium auctor, tincidunt id velit. Suspendisse potenti.

This is an HTML section!   **4**   This is where the table will be placed on the page

This is an HTML subheading!

Lorem ipsum dolor sit amet, consectetur adipiscing elit. sed danibus eros cursus sit amet. Mauris ac ipsum a diam molestie viverra. Fusce non
google.co.uk   vitae in ante. Vestibulum et enim a enim ullamcorper

 HOT TIP: The value of the border attribute is understood to be in pixels; no unit need be provided. If no border is desired the attribute is omitted, not set to "0".

? DID YOU KNOW?
The preferred method of setting pixel width for table borders is with CSS, not with this outmoded table element attribute. If we do not set this attribute now, however, the table may not be visible in all browsers.

? DID YOU KNOW?
You may notice there is nothing on the screen when you save the HTML file and open it in your browser. Don't panic! The table requires more to be visible. This is simply saving 'real estate' on the page where the table will be when we've finished.

Create table rows

The next element in creating a table in HTML is the row element (`<tr></tr>`). Each row is a series of horizontal table data cells, which holds the content. A table can contain any number of rows, and some rows can be used for other purposes such as headers and footers for the table.

1 Open the HTML document with your text editor and save it with a new name.

2 In the body element, add a table (`<table></table>`) element.

3 In the start tag add the following to set the border width to one pixel: border="1"

4 Inside the table element (i.e. between the tags), add four table row (`<tr></tr>`) elements.

5 Save the HTML file and open it in your web browser.

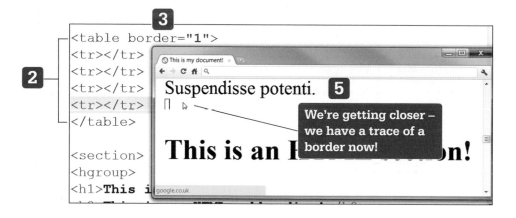

```
<table border="1">
<tr></tr>
<tr></tr>
<tr></tr>
<tr></tr>
</table>

<section>
<hgroup>
<h1>This i
```

Suspendisse potenti.

5 We're getting closer – we have a trace of a border now!

This is an H   n!

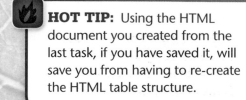

HOT TIP: Using the HTML document you created from the last task, if you have saved it, will save you from having to re-create the HTML table structure.

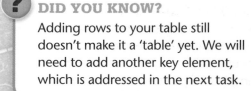

DID YOU KNOW?

Adding rows to your table still doesn't make it a 'table' yet. We will need to add another key element, which is addressed in the next task.

Create table cells

A table's final element is the table data cell, which is created using the `<td></td>` element. Between the tags, the content is added for each cell of the table. A table can have any number of table data cells in each row. The stacks of cells in each row atop each other form columns, making the table complete.

1 Open the HTML document in your text editor.

2 In the `<body>` element, create a `<table>` element with four table row (`<tr></tr>`) elements.

3 Inside each table row element, add three table data (`<td></td>`) elements.

4 Save the HTML document and open it in your web browser.

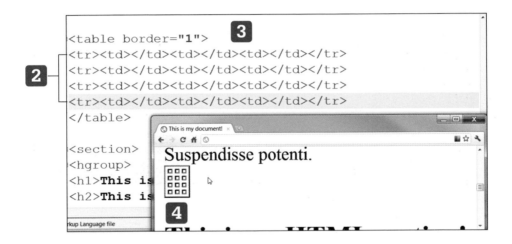

```
<table border="1">   3
<tr><td></td><td></td><td></td></tr>
<tr><td></td><td></td><td></td></tr>
<tr><td></td><td></td><td></td></tr>
<tr><td></td><td></td><td></td></tr>
</table>

<section>
<hgroup>
<h1>This is
<h2>This is
```

Suspendisse potenti.

HOT TIP: Copy and paste one of the `<td></td>` element tag pairs and paste it four times into one table row element; then copy the entire table row element and paste it three more times to create the table quickly.

? DID YOU KNOW?
An HTML table can have other elements along with the table row and table data cell elements. Some of those elements are discussed later in this chapter.

Adjust cell spacing in HTML tables

Cell spacing is the distance between cells in an HTML table. Setting cell spacing can provide clear divisions between cells and make data easier to read. Cell spacing is set using the cellspacing attribute in the start tag of the table element.

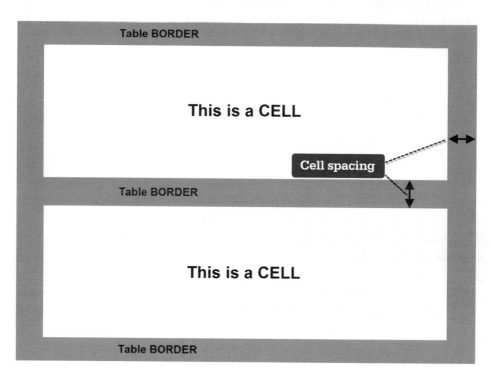

1. Open your HTML file with the table in it in your text editor and save it with a new name.

2. Locate the table element within the body element.

? DID YOU KNOW?

Knowing how to adjust the white space in a table can be helpful, but most formatting for a table is done using CSS now.

3 In the `<table>` element's start tag, add the attribute cellspacing="20".

4 Save the file and open it with your web browser.

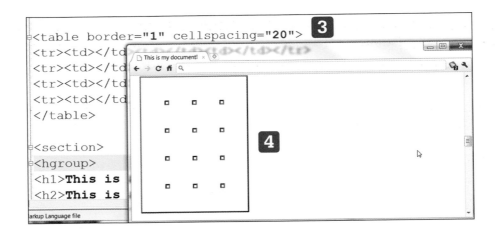

 HOT TIP: The cellspacing attribute is deprecated (being phased out) or obsolete, but is still supported in HTML5. This is true of many other deprecated attributes as well. It is good practice not to form a habit of using those attributes, but knowing they're there if needed is handy as well.

? DID YOU KNOW?

There are other ways to control white space and legibility of data in a table. For instance, using only some of the rules in a grid rather than the full grid can greatly clarify the tabular presentation.

Adjust cell padding in HTML tables

Cell padding is the distance between a cell's content and its border. It is spacing only inside the cell. Cell padding in HTML tables is set with the cellpadding attribute in a table element's start tag. Setting the cellpadding attribute for the table applies to all cells in the table.

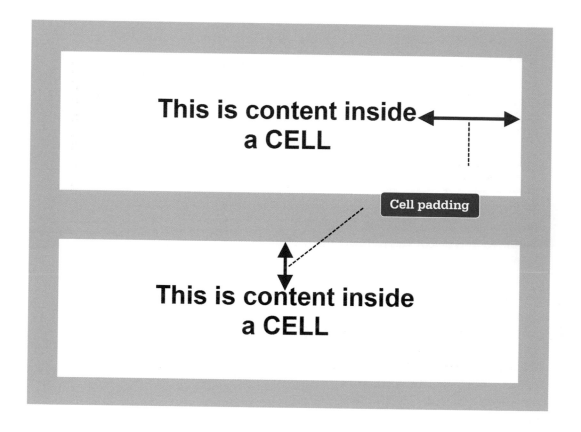

1 Open the HTML document containing the table in your text editor and save it with a new name.

2 In the body element, locate the table element.

3 In the `<table>` element's start tag, add the attribute cellpadding="10". (You can ignore any other attributes if you like.)

4 Save the file and open it with your web browser to view the results.

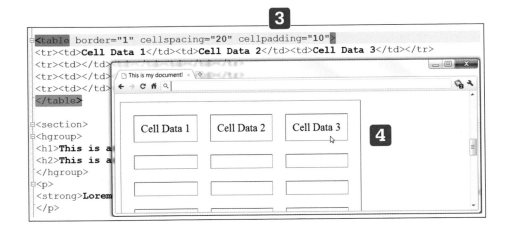

> **! ALERT:** Don't confuse cell padding and cell spacing! Cell spacing is the distance between the edges of each cell; cell padding is the space from the edge of the cell to the content inside the cell.

> **? DID YOU KNOW?**
> As with other aspects of HTML, formatting borders and white space is best left to CSS, but cell padding and spacing are important in the construction of a table so the web designer can decide how best to present data.

Span cells across rows

To have one cell in a table spanning multiple rows, the rowspan attribute of the `<th>` or `<td>` elements creates a larger cell in place of several smaller ones. Like all HTML element attributes, rowspan is entered in the start tag, and the value is the number of rows to span.

1 Open the HTML document with the table in your text editor and save it with a new name.

2 Locate the `<table>` element in the `<body>` element.

3 Add the text 'Cell Data 1' to the first cell, 'Cell Data 2' to the second cell, etc., until the first row is populated.

4 Add the attribute rowspan="2" to the first `<td>` element.

5 In the next row down, *remove* one `<td></td>` element to maintain correct table structure.

6 Save the HTML file and open it in your web browser.

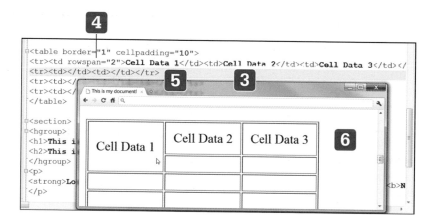

 HOT TIP: Rows can be spanned at will, but the correct number of rows must be omitted or included whenever a cell spans for the structure to be correct.

WHAT DOES THIS MEAN?

Row spanning: crossing over multiple rows with a single data cell in a table.

Span cells across columns

One cell can span multiple columns using the colspan attribute of either the `<th>` `</th>` or `<td></td>` elements. Set the value of the attribute to the number of columns to span and a larger cell will replace smaller ones across multiple columns.

1 Open the HTML document with the populated table in your text editor and save it with a new name.

2 Locate the `<table>` element in the `<body>` element.

3 Add the colspan attribute to the first `<td>` tag (remove any other attributes which may be in the tag) and set the value to "2".

4 Delete the `<td>` element with the 'Cell Data 3' content.

5 Insert a new `<td></td>` element in the next row (if it does not have three in the `<tr></tr>` element).

6 Save the HTML file and open it in your web browser to review the results.

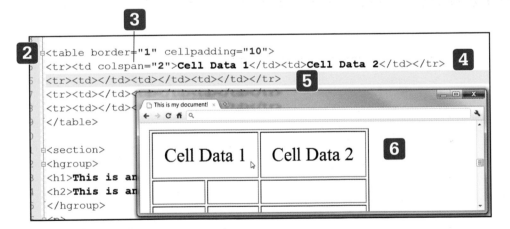

 HOT TIP: Like controlling the white space in a table, controlling column spanning permits you to make tables more visually appealing, and to present data more clearly.

WHAT DOES THIS MEAN?

Column spanning: crossing over multiple columns with a single data cell in a table.

Create table row headings

Table headings are rows or groups of rows used as row titles. Generally a header describes the tabular data it heads. The text might be emboldened or emphasised to make it stand out from the tabular data.

Table headers are marked up a couple of different ways in HTML, depending on the type of heading.

To create a row header, use the `<th>...</th>` element instead of the `<td></td>` element to designate the heading.

1 Open the HTML document with the table in your text editor and save it with a new name.

2 In the table element, remove the cellspacing attribute.

3 In the first row, change the first `<td></td>` element to a `<th></th>` element (change both tags).

4 Between the `<th></th>` tags, add some text (any brief snippet will work).

5 Add data to the rest of the cells in that row.

6 Save the HTML file and open it in your web browser.

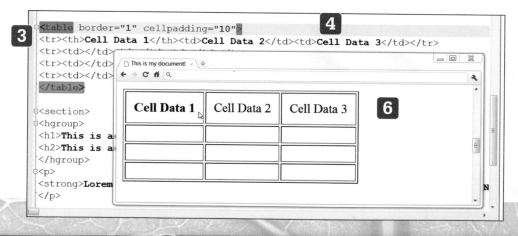

ALERT: *Only* change the *first* `<td></td>` element to the `<th></th>` element!

DID YOU KNOW?

Row headings are generally at the far left of the row which they head. Row headings can be used to create a grid, such as sales figures tracked year-to-year on a quarterly basis. In such cases, use of empty cells as placeholders is beneficial.

Create table column headings

Column headings are the top cells in a column which serve to describe, or head, tabular columns rather than rows. Use the `<thead></thead>` element in place of the `<tr></tr>` element to group a row of cells into a column heading row.

1 Open the HTML file with the table in it using your text editor and save it with a new name.

2 Change the first `<tr>` element to `<thead>`; change the end tag as well.

3 Change the `<td>` elements to `<th>` elements in this row, making sure to change the end tags as well.

4 Save the HTML file and open it in your web browser and note the heavier border under the first row of cells.

The `<thead>` element by itself has no visual impact on a table without borders. To see this, fill the other cells of your table with data (any data will do) and remove the border attribute from the `<table>` tag. Save the file and re-open it in your web browser. There is no distinction between the heading cells and the others. The `<th>` element adds formatting to the content. The `<theader>` is largely a *grouping* element, which can have formatting applied to it using CSS. The `<thead>` element tells the browser which rows are included in the heading.

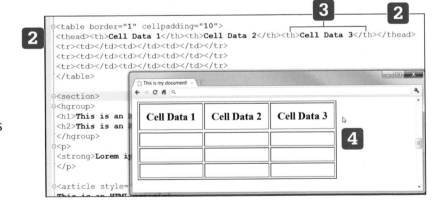

? DID YOU KNOW?

A non-breaking space is a special character you can use in the cell, which doesn't cause the character to display but isn't seen as empty by the browser. A non-breaking space is created with the ampersand symbol (&) followed by the characters "nbsp" (without the quote marks, of course), and a semi-colon, hence:

► SEE ALSO: Table headings are discussed in the 'Create a table heading' section, next.

Create a table heading

To create a row or multiple rows for a table heading, use the `<thead></thead>` element to enclose the rows you want as the heading. While this has little visual impact on the table, it does instruct the browser to use those rows as a heading for the table and formatting in CSS can be applied to all the rows at once by formatting the `<thead></thead>` element.

1 Open your HTML file with the table in it and save it with a new name.

2 Replace the first row's `<tr>` (the *start tag only*) with the `<thead>` tag (if it's not already changed).

3 Add text content to all the cells in the table; simple alpha or numeric data will suffice.

4 Replace the *second row's* `</tr>` (closing tag) with the `</thead>` tag (closing tag).

5 Save the file, open it in your web browser and note the heavier border under the second row of cells.

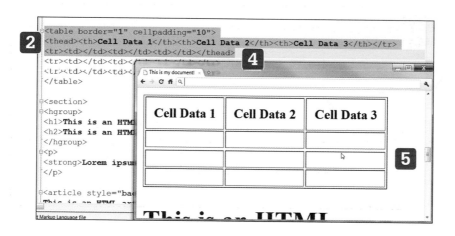

? DID YOU KNOW?

For most purposes, CSS is the preferred method of formatting for HTML elements. While the `<thead>` element provides a visual cue to its purpose if the table is bordered, most of its purpose lies in grouping the heading rows together as a unit.

HOT TIP: You can populate tables with 'Lorem ipsum' text or with copy and paste to speed up the process.

Form a table body

HTML allows you to designate a block of rows and columns as the table body using the `<tbody>` element. The `<tbody>` element must come after `<thead>` elements in a table (if they're used) but before any `<tr>` elements outside of headings. It must come before any table footer element (`<tfooter></tfooter>`) used as well.

1 Open the HTML document with the table in it in your text editor and save it with a new name.

2 Change the first row to a header row by changing the `<tr></tr>` element to `<thead></thead>` (remove all other `<thead></thead>` elements if they exist).

3 Insert the `<tbody>` start tag on a blank line under the `<thead>` row.

4 Locate the `</table>` tag and insert a blank before it.

5 On the newly created blank line, add the `</tbody>` closing tag.

6 Save the HTML file and open it in your web browser.

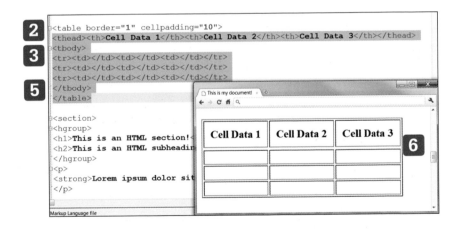

```
<table border="1" cellpadding="10">
<thead><th>Cell Data 1</th><th>Cell Data 2</th><th>Cell Data 3</th></thead>
<tbody>
<tr><td></td><td></td><td></td></tr>
<tr><td></td><td></td><td></td></tr>
<tr><td></td><td></td><td></td></tr>
</tbody>
</table>

<section>
<hgroup>
<h1>This is an HTML section!<
<h2>This is an HTML subheadin
</hgroup>
<p>
<strong>Lorem ipsum dolor sit
</p>
```

Markup Language file

Cell Data 1	Cell Data 2	Cell Data 3

▶ **SEE ALSO:** See the 'Create a table footer' section, next, for more information on the `<tfooter>` element.

? DID YOU KNOW?
Don't be surprised if you don't see a dramatic change in your table's appearance. The `<tbody>` element doesn't have any visual effect unless it's formatted with CSS.

Create a table footer

Table footers are rows which summarise the column information above them, or are footnotes for tabular data. They display at the bottom of a table and must come after any `<thead>` or `<caption>` elements, but before `<tbody>` or ungrouped `<tr>` elements. The footer is specified with the `<tfoot>` element, and can contain any number of rows.

1 In your text editor, open the HTML document with the table and save it with a new name.

2 Locate the `<thead>` element and add a blank line under it.

3 On the new line, add a `<tfoot>` element.

4 In the `<tfoot>` element, insert one row element and three data cell elements inside the row.

5 Add cell content of 'Footer Cell 1', 'Footer Cell 2' and 'Footer Cell 3' to each respective cell.

6 Save the HTML file and open it in your web browser; note the heavier border before the footer cells.

 HOT TIP: Remember to use copy and paste to populate sample data or clone elements in an HTML document.

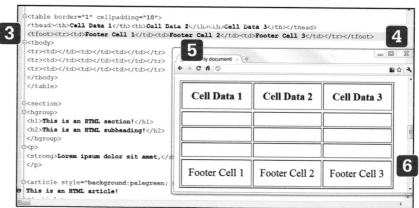

? DID YOU KNOW?
Because HTML tables do not require a footer, both the start and end tags for the `<tfoot>` element are considered and listed as optional in the World Wide Web Consortium online documentation.

? DID YOU KNOW?
HTML table footers are just like any other HTML element, and can be formatted independently of the table with CSS.

Add a caption to a table

The caption (`<caption></caption>`) element names tables as illustrative figures and provides captions. It must be the first element inside the `<table>` element or it may not be displayed, or may display incorrectly. The caption element can contain other elements, such as `<p>` elements. The caption element may format the caption text, depending on browser interpretation.

1 Open the HTML document with the table in your text editor and save it with a new name.

2 Under the `<table>` element and before the `<thead>` start tag, add the `<caption>` element.

3 Inside the caption element, add an `<h5>` element with 'Test Table Caption' between the tags. (Don't forget to close the `<h5>` element!)

4 Under the `<h5>` element, add a `<p>` element and some descriptive text. Use 'Lorem ipsum' text if you like. (Close the `<p>` element!)

5 Save the HTML file and load it into your web browser to view the results.

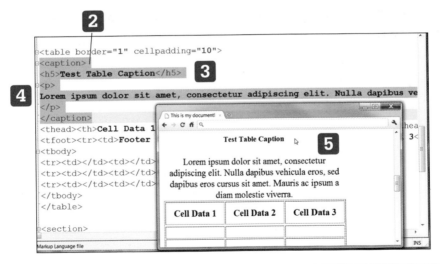

HOT TIP: The specification for HTML5 requires the caption element to be the first element in a table, but in some browsers, it renders correctly even if it's misplaced (see the screenshot above). It is always recommended you follow the specifications for a given element to be sure the web page renders correctly.

? **DID YOU KNOW?**

Remember, the `<caption>` element doesn't apply specific formatting: it tells the browser how it should interpret the content in the tag. The interpretation of that tag is left to the browser manufacturer. It is possible, if unlikely, that Opera, Internet Explorer and Safari will all interpret the same tag differently. So don't expect a certain type of formatting unless you are specifically applying a format to text content.

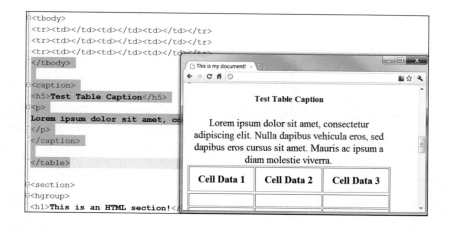

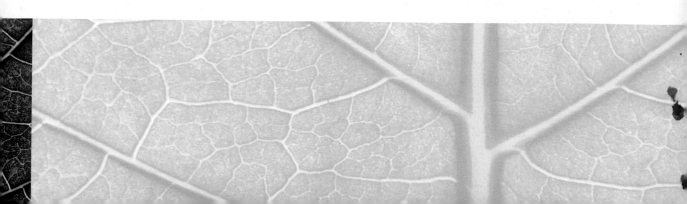

6 Working with HTML forms and attributes

Introduction

HTML forms contain the controls which collect user data and transmit the gathered information to a web server for processing. There are several steps required to set up an HTML form. Those steps can be performed in any order, but all must exist for the form to work. Those steps are:

- creating the user interface, or what the user sees and interacts with

- setting up the user input processing on the web server and

- establishing communications between the user interface and the web server.

HTML5 is more than just a new set of elements and tags, though. There are also fresh attributes which assist in making web pages a new experience. These new attributes make HTML forms better, clearer and more accessible than ever before.

Build a simple HTML form

HTML forms are created with the `<form>` element. The form element groups together all other form elements, such as the form controls. Form elements cannot be nested, but multiple forms can exist on an HTML page. HTML forms use controls to gather user input and data. Form controls include things like text boxes, radio (or option) buttons and checkboxes (or tickboxes).

All the other elements for the form are contained within the form element. Those are the elements which a user can see; the `<form>` element itself is not a visible element.

1. Create a new HTML document using the instructions from Chapter 2.

2. Add a `<title>` element with 'My First HTML Form!' as the title content.

3. In the `<body>` element, add a `<form>` element. Include both tags.

4. Save the HTML file and open it with your web browser: note nothing is visible!

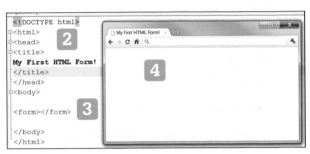

? DID YOU KNOW?

Because forms are complex and can do almost anything with user data – calculate a cost, perform a search, create an account, return search results, etc. – the full functionality of forms goes beyond the scope of this book.

? DID YOU KNOW?

Different forms on the same HTML page must have different names set in the name attribute start tag. If one form on a web page appears to collect different data types – like a customer information form for customer data and an order information form about a customer's order – it may actually be different forms.

🔥 HOT TIP: Like most other HTML elements, the `<form>` element has several attributes which can be set in the start tag. The form name, the `charset` attribute, and even `autocomplete` on or off can all be set with attributes in the `<form>` element's start tag.

⚠ ALERT: Details of the protocols used to send and receive data over the Internet, including in-depth details of the get and post methods, are beyond the scope of this book. Information about these topics is available online for further study.

Set method and action attributes

The method attribute designates which protocol is used to send the data to the web server. While there are four settings for the method attribute, we are interested only in the post method for our purposes. The post method tells the HTML form to use the Post protocol. The form puts all the data collected into a data packet with an HTTP header and sends it to the web server.

1 Open the HTML form document you created in your text editor.

2 In the `<form>` element start tag, add the method attribute and set the value to post.

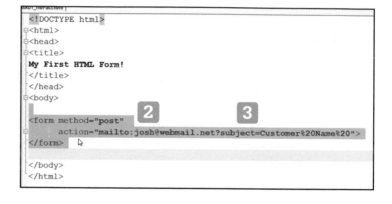

```
<!DOCTYPE html>
<html>
<head>
<title>
My First HTML Form!
</title>
</head>
<body>

                                    2                      3
<form method="post"
      action="mailto:josh@webmail.net?subject=Customer%20Name%20">
</form>

</body>
</html>
```

3 Add the action attribute and assign the value as follows:
"mailto:youremailaddress@email.com?subject=Customer%20Name%20" (Use your actual email address if possible.)

4 Add the enctype (encryption text) attribute after the action attribute; separate them by a space.

5 Set the enctype value to text/plain (use double quotes as with all other HTML attribute values).

6 Save the HTML file. You may open it in your web browser though nothing is visible yet.

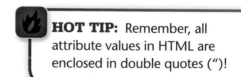

HOT TIP: Remember, all attribute values in HTML are enclosed in double quotes (")!

ALERT: If you can't use an actual email address for this exercise, the "mailto" protocol won't work properly.

HOT TIP: Getting a button to work isn't dependent entirely on the button. It's also dependent on the form, and the method/action assignment we provide. The form's method and action attributes must be set for the button to be able to function.

Use the fieldset element

Several controls on a form can be grouped together visually with the `<fieldset>` element. They can also be given a common name to group them functionally. The `<fieldset>` element draws a box around the form elements inside it. This makes it useful for defining related areas of a form or related controls.

1 Open the HTML form document you created with your text editor.

2 In the `<form>` element, add a `<fieldset>` element.

3 Inside the `<fieldset>` element, add an `<h5>` element with the content 'Placeholder'.

4 Save the HTML form and open it in your web browser.

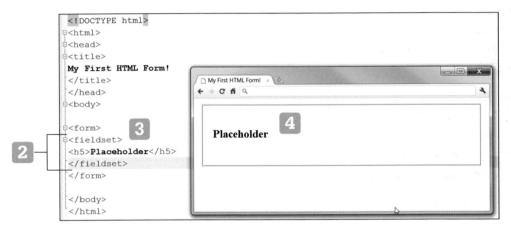

```
<!DOCTYPE html>
<html>
<head>
<title>
My First HTML Form!
</title>
</head>
<body>

<form>
<fieldset>
  <h5>Placeholder</h5>
</fieldset>
</form>

</body>
</html>
```

? **DID YOU KNOW?**
The `<fieldset>` element is only a logical grouping for HTML controls. It does not add functionality to anything on the form, only providing visual cues to related items.

HOT TIP: Use the `<fieldset>` element to draw a viewer's eye to clusters of controls, and to manipulate white space.

HOT TIP: The `<fieldset>` element requires an end tag as part of its construct.

Use the legend element

The `<legend>` element is used to provide the display name, similar to a `<caption>` element for a table. The `<legend>` element, when used with the `<fieldset>` element, provides a name to the logical grouping of controls on an HTML form. The `<legend>` element must go inside the `<fieldset>` element it applies to.

1 Open the HTML form in your text editor.

2 In the `<fieldset>` element, create a blank line under the start tag.

3 Add the `<legend>` tag (both start and end tags) with the content 'Group Name'.

4 Save the HTML form and open it in your web browser.

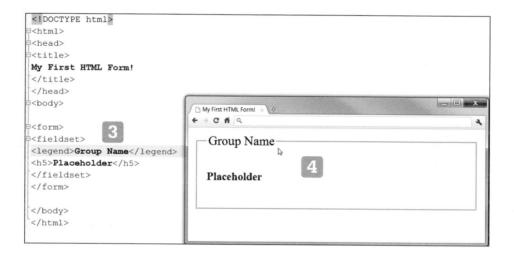

```
<!DOCTYPE html>
<html>
<head>
<title>
My First HTML Form!
</title>
</head>
<body>

<form>
<fieldset>          3
<legend>Group Name</legend>
<h5>Placeholder</h5>
</fieldset>
</form>

</body>
</html>
```

My First HTML Form!

Group Name
  Placeholder   4

? DID YOU KNOW?
Different browsers may handle the `<fieldset>` element differently behind the scenes, so be sure to follow the standards from the WHATWG when using it to provide consistent behaviour and display across platforms.

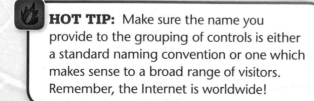

HOT TIP: Make sure the name you provide to the grouping of controls is either a standard naming convention or one which makes sense to a broad range of visitors. Remember, the Internet is worldwide!

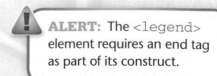

ALERT: The `<legend>` element requires an end tag as part of its construct.

Label HTML form controls

Use the HTML `<label>` element to place a label on the web page for any control. The user cannot interact with a label, and a label does not return or receive any data. It's just a little sign or stamp on the page indicating what the control is called. Labels can provide information on what the user needs to do with the control as well.

1 Open the HTML document with the form on it with your text editor.

2 In the `<fieldset>` element, add the `<label>` element under the `<h5>` element.

3 Add the text 'Label 1', followed by the `</label>` end tag.

4 Save the HTML file and open it in your web browser.

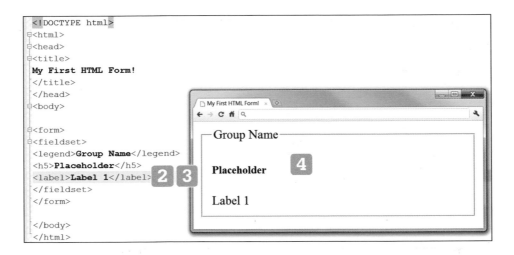

HOT TIP: A `<label>` element requires both a start and an end tag to indicate the label content to the browser.

DID YOU KNOW?
The label appears where the text falls in the `<label>` element's content; if a control element precedes the label text content, the label shows to the *right* of the control. If a control element follows the label, the label displays to the *left* of the control.

DID YOU KNOW?
Labels can be explicitly associated with either forms or controls. If the `<label>` element's form attribute is set to the form's name, the label is explicitly associated with the form. If the `for` attribute of the `<label>` element is set to a control element ID, it is explicitly associated with that control.

Add buttons to an HTML form

Button controls on HTML forms are created with the `<button>` element. Attributes identify and label the button, and set how it behaves. The button can even be disabled (or 'greyed out') on a form until certain conditions are met.

Adding a `<button>` element is simple; having a button perform an action is more complex. In most cases, a scripting language controls what happens when the button is clicked. A button can be made into a reset button or a submit button, however, using the type attribute.

1 Open the HTML form document in your text editor.

  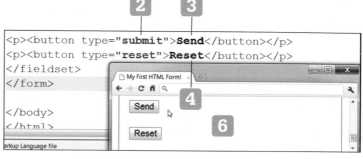

```
<p><button type="submit">Send</button></p>
<p><button type="reset">Reset</button></p>
</fieldset>
</form>

</body>
</html>
```
arkup Language file

2 Add a button element to the `<fieldset>` element and set the type attribute to Submit.

3 Add the word 'Send' between the button element's tags.

4 Add another button element, set the type attribute to Reset and put 'Reset' between the tags.

5 Surround the button elements with paragraph elements.

6 Save the HTML file and load it in your web browser to view the results.

? DID YOU KNOW?
Most HTML controls can be set to be disabled until certain conditions are met or other controls contain data.

? DID YOU KNOW?
Getting a button to work isn't just dependent on the button. We must set the form's method and action attributes for the button to be able to do what it must do.

! ALERT: Add the method=post attribute to the `<form>` element start tag if it's not already there.

WHAT DOES THIS MEAN?

Disabled: when a field or control on an HTML form, or a section of a form, is not available for user interaction. Generally certain conditions must be met or data provided to enable the disabled control(s).

Add a selection list to an HTML form

The `<select>` element creates a drop-down selection list. The size attribute specifies how many list options to show, and must be greater than zero. The multiple attribute allows selection of more than one item from the list.

Use `<select>` with the `<options>` element. `<options>` provides the list from which to choose. An `<optgroup>` element can be used to group together a series of `<option>` elements under a common label which is displayed in the drop-down list. The label attribute, enclosed in double quotes, is what shows as a label.

1 Open the HTML form document in your text editor and save it with a new name.

2 In the form element, add a `<select>` element without the multiple attribute.

3 Inside the `<select>` element, add an `<optgroup>` element with the label attribute: 'colour'.

4 Inside the `<optgroup>` element add three `<option>` elements with the text 'Red', 'Blue' and 'Yellow' inside them.

5 Add a `<label>` element before the `<select>` element with text content 'Colours'.

6 Save the HTML file and open it in your web browser.

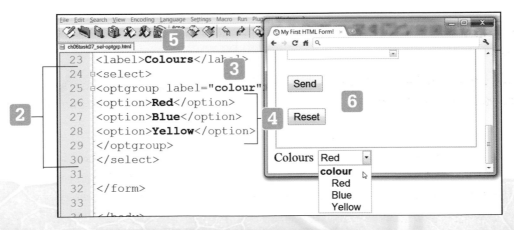

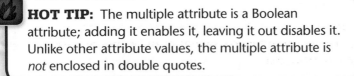

HOT TIP: The multiple attribute is a Boolean attribute; adding it enables it, leaving it out disables it. Unlike other attribute values, the multiple attribute is *not* enclosed in double quotes.

Add text area HTML controls

The `<textarea>` element provides a large input area for text data. A text area is a multi-line plain text entry area which can hold a lot of text. If the text area is made read-only, it can be used to present information in a confined area on the page. It can also be left editable to provide a place for more detailed user input than text fields permit.

The `<textarea>` element allows control over how many characters to allow per line with the cols attribute, set to a non-zero integer. Determine how many lines to present onscreen with the rows attribute. You can limit the amount of data in the `<textarea>` element with the maxlength attribute.

1 Open the HTML form with your text editor.

2 Insert a `<textarea>` element with the rows attribute to 10 and the cols attribute to 30.

3 Add the text 'This is a text area!' between the tags.

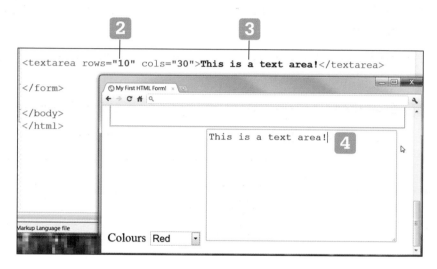

4 Save the HTML file and open it in your web browser.

5 Type some multi-line text into the text area to ensure it functions correctly.

? DID YOU KNOW?

There are many other attributes and associated settings required with `<textarea>` elements, and they are detailed in the WHATWG's online documentation at http://whatwg.org/.

HOT TIP: Note that both a start and end tag are required for a `<textarea>` element. Any text content between the tags is used as initial text in the field. This is *not* the same as placeholder text, however, which is what appears in a field until the user enters the field.

Add checkbox controls to a form

Checkboxes are among the most common form controls used. They allow users to mark selections from a list or group of choices where more than one is appropriate (such as a 'Check all that apply' area of a form). Checkboxes are generally square on the screen, and are created using the `<input />` element with a type attribute of checkbox.

1 Open the HTML form document with your text editor.

2 Create a `<fieldset>` element with a `<legend>` element containing the text 'Checkbox Array'.

3 In the `<fieldset>`, add three `<input />` controls and set the type attribute to checkbox.

4 Add a label for each control, naming them 'Checkbox 1', 'Checkbox 2' and 'Checkbox 3' respectively.

5 Save the HTML document and open it in your web browser.

6 Test each checkbox by clicking it to tick or untick it.

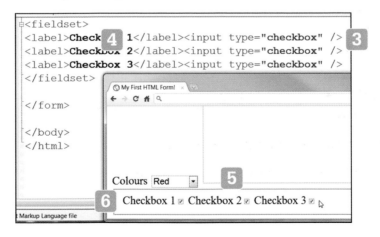

HOT TIP: You can copy and paste the existing `<input />` elements and simply edit the type attributes in each. Remember, copy and paste is your friend when doing repetitive markup.

? DID YOU KNOW?

Spelling counts with any markup, scripting or coding language, and HTML is no exception. The spellings for all attributes, unless otherwise noted, are US spellings. If you're unsure how to spell an attribute, value or tag, you can check the World Hypertext Application Technology Work Group's documentation online at http://whatwg.org.

Add radio buttons to a form

Radio buttons, or option buttons, are on-or-off clickable controls which permit only one selection from the group of available choices. Radio buttons are used together when a single choice from several is required ('Yes' or 'No' agreement sections of licence agreements, for instance). Radio buttons are often grouped in an option group to make the choices clearer for users. Radio buttons are created with the `<input />` element by setting the type attribute to radio.

1 Open the HTML form document in your text editor.

2 Create a `<fieldset>` element with a `<legend>` element containing the text 'Radio Buttons'.

3 Create three `<input />` elements and set the type attribute to "radio" for all three.

4 Add name attributes to each with values of 'Radio 1', 'Radio 2' and 'Radio 3'.

5 Add `<label>` elements in front of each with text content matching the control name.

6 Save the HTML document and open it in your web browser.

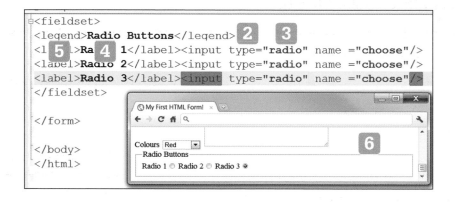

HOT TIP: A web browser knows any radio buttons with the same name are mutually exclusive, i.e. only one of them can be active or clicked. Clicking one automatically clears the others of the same name.

ALERT: Don't forget to close the structural elements such as the `<fieldset>` elements with end tags, and in the `<legend>` elements will require end tags also. The `<input />` tag is an open tag and doesn't require an end tag.

Add placeholder text in HTML form controls

Placeholder text is text which appears by default in an empty control, before any input. HTML5 provides the placeholder attribute for several controls, such as text boxes and text areas. Add the placeholder attribute to the element's start tag, with whatever you'd like the placeholder text to say enclosed in double quotes, and the browser will display it in the control on the page.

1 In your text editor, open the HTML form document.

2 Locate or create the `<input />` element of type "text".

```
<p><input type="text" name="text" placeholder="Text box"/></p>
<p><input t  4 "email" name="email" placeholder="Enter email"/></p>
<p><input ty  "tel" name="tel" placeholder="Phone"/></p>
<p><input
<p><button
<p><button
</fieldset

<label>Col
<select>

Markup Language file
```

My First HTM

Text box

Enter email

Phone

3 Add the placeholder attribute with the value "Text box".

4 Locate the `<input />` element of type "email" and add the placeholder attribute with the value "Enter email".

5 Locate the `<input />` element of type "tel" and add the placeholder text "Phone".

6 Save the HTML file and open it with your browser.

 HOT TIP: Not all browsers support the placeholder attribute functionality. If you can't see the placeholder text, try downloading a newer version of your browser or a different, HTML5-compliant browser.

? DID YOU KNOW?
HTML5 form controls which may need it, like text boxes, email address fields or URL fields, can contain placeholder text to improve the user interface.

WHAT DOES THIS MEAN?

Placeholder text: text which appears in a form field as a descriptor until the user enters the field for data entry. Placeholder text can be anything and is often used to specify the type of information required for the data input.

Set a field to autofocus

Use the autofocus attribute to set the focus to a control on a form when the page loads. This can be important when the order of information input is critical, such as with a password-protected form which requires a password first. The autofocus attribute is Boolean, so including it in the element turns it on while excluding it leaves it off. All HTML5 controls can use the autofocus attribute.

1 Open the HTML form document with your text editor.

2 Locate or create a `<textarea>` element on the form.

3 In the start tag, add the autofocus attribute.

4 Save the HTML document and open it in your web browser to see that the cursor is placed in the text area by default.

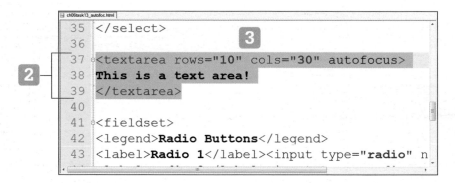

? **DID YOU KNOW?**

As technology changes, HTML adapts to accommodate the changes. For example, one of HTML5's advantages is how the elements work for handheld devices. The iPhone, for example, will place a special keyboard onscreen with a small space bar and a prominent @ sign to make entering an email address easier when it encounters an `email <input />` element in a web page. Email addresses do not have spaces as a general rule, but almost all of them have the @ symbol in them. The iPhone also customises the keyboard for a `url` `<input />` element, providing a prominent 'dot' key rather than a standard keyboard.

WHAT DOES THIS MEAN?

Focus: placing the cursor into a particular object, such as a field or form control, for input.

7 Using more HTML input controls

Introduction

Text boxes for input from a user are marked up with the `<input />` tag, but the use of the `<input />` tag in HTML5 is much more extensive than that. It has more than a dozen new type definitions, which means it's able to represent more than a dozen controls. Things such as password fields, phone number fields, email address fields, and many others can all be created with the `<input />` tag, and all by simply setting the type attribute to the appropriate control.

Because of its versatility and wide use, the `<input />` tag deserves a chapter of its own. If you have not worked through Chapter 6, 'Working with HTML forms and attributes', you should do so now. You will need the HTML form created in that chapter for use with the exercises in this chapter.

The `<input />` element is an empty element, meaning there is no closing tag. A trailing slash is used in the start tag, along with all the attributes to set the display for the browser. Since it's an open tag, the reference to the `<input />` element and `<input />` tag are synonymous.

Create an HTML text box control

Text box controls are marked up with the `<input />` tag by setting the type attribute to "text". The text box created is a clear-text input field which receives free input from users. When using more than one plain text field on a form, identify them with the name or id attributes for distinction.

1 Open the HTML form document you created in Chapter 6 with your text editor.

2 Add an `<input />` tag to the `<form>` element.

3 Set the type attribute to "text": `<input type="text" />`

4 Place a `<p>` element around the `<input />` tag.

5 Add a `<label>` element after the `<p>` start tag, with the content text 'Text Field' between them.

6 Save the HTML file and open it in your web browser.

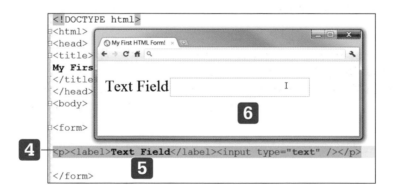

DID YOU KNOW?

A text box is a basic text input field and should not be used to collect extensive data. To gather significant amounts of data, or to present areas where larger input is required, use a `<textarea>` element. See the 'Add text area HTML controls' section of Chapter 6 for more information.

DID YOU KNOW?

Not all browsers can properly display all input tags. In the event a browser doesn't recognise the type attribute, it displays the control as a text box, a default fall-back position. This ensures all browsers handle HTML5 forms without errors.

Create a search field

Search fields allow users to search for the text they enter in the field. The entry is used as the search parameter when the search is run. To create a search box, set the `<input />` control type value to "search".

1 Open the HTML form document you created in Chapter 6 with your text editor.

2 Add an `<input />` tag to the `<form>` element.

3 Set the type attribute to "search": `<input type="search" />`

4 Place a `<p>` element around the `<input />` tag.

5 Add a `<label>` element after the `<p>` start tag, with the content text 'Search Field' between them.

6 Save the HTML file and open it in your web browser.

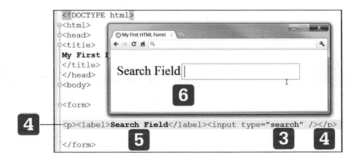

4 ───

 DID YOU KNOW?
Since most browsers won't render the search box differently from a normal text box, it may be a good idea to add a submit button to the form to initiate the search. See the 'Add buttons to an HTML form' section of Chapter 6 for more information.

 HOT TIP: At the time of writing, not all browsers handle the "search" setting in a unique way for the `<input />` tag. Only the browsers based on WebKit, such as Safari and Safari for Windows, make use of the search field in a visual way. In most browsers, the search box is rendered exactly like a normal text box.

Create a telephone number field

One of the new things HTML5 provides with the `<input />` tag is the telephone number field. It allows specifically for input of a telephone number to a field rather than requiring a text field. The telephone number field is marked up by using the `<input />` tag's type setting of "tel".

1 Open the HTML form document in your text editor.

2 Add an `<input />` element to the `<form>` element.

3 Set the `<input />` element's type attribute to "tel".

4 Add a `<label>` element with text content 'Phone Number'.

5 Enclose both the `<input />` tag and `<label>` element in a `<p>` element.

6 Save the HTML document and open it in your web browser.

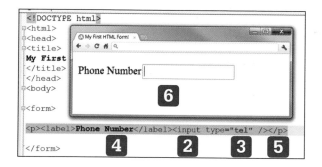

 ALERT: Formatting the phone number to look like a phone number is best done with CSS, rather than HTML.

 DID YOU KNOW?

How the input from a particular control looks on the form may not be different from one type setting to another, but how the input is *interpreted* is different. The type attribute tells the browser, form and server what sort of input that field contains. Use the different type settings with caution!

Create a password field

A password field is a text field which obscures the entry as the user types. It replaces the text with either asterisks (*) or bullet points. The point is to offer security, and password fields are used almost everywhere on the Internet. Anywhere a log-in is required, the password field will be seen. It's created with an `<input />` element of type attribute password.

1 Open the HTML form document with your text editor.

2 Add an `<input />` element at the top of the `<form>` element with the type "password".

3 Place a label element in front of the `<input />` element with the text 'Password' in it.

4 Enclose both elements in a `<p>` element.

5 Save the HTML form and open it in your web browser.

6 Type a word into the field to see it obscure the text.

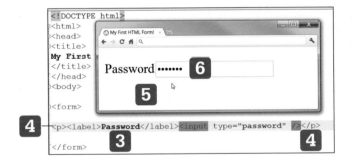

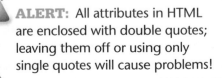

ALERT: All attributes in HTML are enclosed with double quotes; leaving them off or using only single quotes will cause problems!

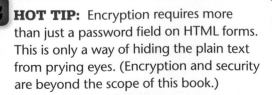

HOT TIP: Encryption requires more than just a password field on HTML forms. This is only a way of hiding the plain text from prying eyes. (Encryption and security are beyond the scope of this book.)

Create a spinbox control

Spinboxes are number selectors which have an up and a down arrow to choose a number from a range. They are created with the `<input />` tag's type attribute set to "number" and with the "min" and "max" attributes set to whole numbers so the choices are limited. For instance, set the min value to 1 and the max value to 5 to present the user with a spinbox which goes from 1 to 5.

1 Open the HTML form document in your text editor.

2 Add an `<input />` element to the `<form>` element.

3 Set the `<input />` element's type attribute to "number", the min attribute to "1" and the max to "5".

4 Add a `<label>` element with text content 'Number'.

5 Enclose both the `<input />` tag and `<label>` element within a `<p>` element.

6 Save the HTML document and open it in your web browser.

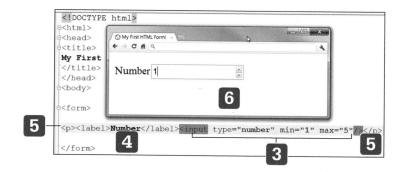

5 `<p><label>Number</label><input type="number" min="1" max="5" /></p>`
4 **3** **5**

ALERT: The choices in a spinbox will be unlimited if you don't set the "min" and "max" attributes!

HOT TIP: You can copy and paste the `<input />` tag when you have many controls on a form to create and simply change the appropriate attributes, such as type, name or id, to create new controls.

Create an HTML file picker control

A file picker is a special field which opens a dialogue box to browse for and select a file to upload from the local computer. The file picker is used wherever a file from the local machine is stored on the web server. The `<input />` element's type attribute is set to file to create the file picker.

1 Open the HTML form document in your text editor.

2 Add an `<input />` element to the `<form>` element.

3 Set the `<input />` element's type attribute to "file".

4 Add a `<label>` element with text content 'File Picker' and enclose both with a `<p>` element.

5 Save the HTML document and open it in your web browser.

6 Test the file picker in your web browser (but don't try to upload a file!).

? DID YOU KNOW?

The file picker control launches the file dialogue box so you can navigate to the file you'd like to upload.

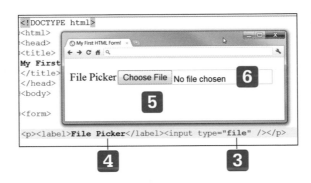

```
<!DOCTYPE html>
<html>
<head>
<title>
My First
</title>
</head>
<body>

<form>

<p><label>File Picker</label><input type="file" /></p>
```

? DID YOU KNOW?

File pickers were not available prior to HTML5. If your web browser of choice isn't at its latest version, it may not be able to properly display the file picker control. It will most likely default to displaying the control as a text box.

HOT TIP: Other factors – not the least of which is a web server – are required to be able to upload a file to a web server. This task shows only how the control on an HTML form is created.

Create a range slider control

The `<input />` tag's "range" type creates a slider control, where a slider is moved between a range of numbers. Like a spinbox, the range control has "min" and "max" attributes to set the limits of the control. The slider allows selection by use of the slider bar rather than a spinbox, but the concept is the same for both.

1 Open the HTML form document in your text editor.

2 Add an `<input />` element to the `<form>` element.

3 Set the `<input />` element's type attribute to "range", the min attribute to "1" and the max to "5".

4 Add a `<label>` element with text content 'Slider'.

5 Enclose both the `<input />` tag and `<label>` element within a `<p>` element.

6 Save the HTML document and open it in your web browser.

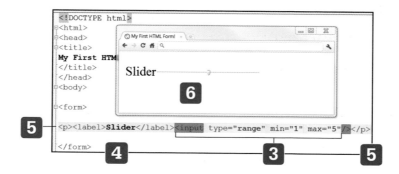

DID YOU KNOW?

For the time being, the way slider controls are rendered makes it more judicious and easier from the user's perspective to simply use a spinbox control, rather than the range slider. While the value is the same, there is nothing to indicate to the user what value they have selected, or what the choice range is. Browser support may improve in the future, but at the time of writing, the slider control simply isn't a good option, even if it is a 'cool' feature in HTML5.

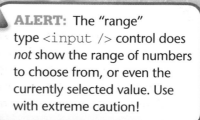

ALERT: The "range" type `<input />` control does *not* show the range of numbers to choose from, or even the currently selected value. Use with extreme caution!

Create a URL field control

A URL field is a text field specifically for the input of a web address. It's created by using the "url" setting for the type attribute in an `<input />` tag. The kind of information placed in the field is validated by the form when submitted.

1 Open the HTML form document in your text editor.

2 Add an `<input />` element to the `<form>` element.

3 Set the `<input />` element's type attribute to "url".

4 Add a `<label>` element with text content 'Web Address'.

5 Enclose both the `<input />` tag and `<label>` element within a `<p>` element.

6 Save the HTML document and open it in your web browser.

 HOT TIP: Not all browsers will display the URL field in a unique or visibly identifiable way. The Apple iPhone Safari browser, however, adjusts the onscreen keyboard when it encounters a URL field.

 DID YOU KNOW?

Because HTML forms look at the type attribute of each control on the form, they can identify the type of information each field is intended to hold. The form can validate the type of information in each field as it's submitted to a web server to ensure it's all correct.

Create an email address control

Setting an `<input />` tag's type attribute to "email" tells the browser and form the field should contain an email address. The field is specific to containing email addresses. The form validates the data type when it is submitted.

1 Open the HTML form document in your text editor.

2 Add an `<input />` element to the `<form>` element.

3 Set the `<input />` element's type attribute to "email".

4 Add a `<label>` element with text content 'Email'.

5 Enclose both the `<input />` tag and `<label>` element within a `<p>` element.

6 Save the HTML document and open it in your web browser.

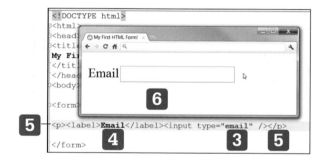

? **DID YOU KNOW?**

The Apple iPhone version of the Safari browser will change the onscreen keyboard to provide email-specific keys when an email field is encountered.

WHAT DOES THIS MEAN?

Data validation: confirmation that data contained in the fields of a form is the correct data type: for example, that an email field contains an email address.

Create a date picker

A date picker is a fully functional feature in HTML5 created by setting the `<input />` tag type to "date". The date picker (or chooser) allows a date to be selected from a calendar pop-up object when it's activated. The type setting "date" provides a selection of day, month and year.

1 Open the HTML form document in your text editor.

2 Add an `<input />` element to the `<form>` element.

3 Set the `<input />` element's type attribute to "date".

4 Add a `<label>` element with text content 'Date'.

5 Enclose both the `<input />` tag and `<label>` element within a `<p>` element.

6 Save the HTML document and open it in your web browser.

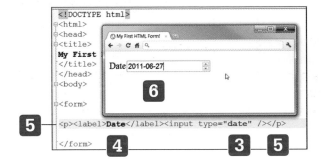

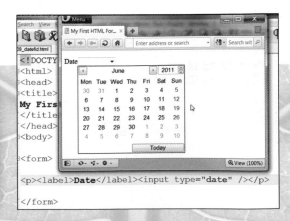

? DID YOU KNOW?

Not all browsers display the pop-up calendar object shown in the screenshot above. The screenshot opposite shows the date control as it is displayed in Google Chrome.

Create a colour picker

Choosing colours from the standard Windows-style dialogue box in the browser window is now possible with the "color" type attribute setting for the `<input />` tag. By clicking on the colour chooser, the user is presented with the standard colours available to the browser. Clicking on the 'Other…' button brings up the colour choice dialogue box for more options.

1 Open the HTML form document in your text editor.

2 Add an `<input />` element to the `<form>` element.

3 Set the `<input />` element's type attribute to "color".

4 Add a `<label>` element with text content 'Colour'.

5 Enclose both the `<input />` tag and `<label>` element within a `<p>` element.

6 Save the HTML document and open it in your web browser.

? DID YOU KNOW?
While the type attribute value must have a US spelling to function, the label can contain a UK spelling with no ill effects. It is, after all, just a label.

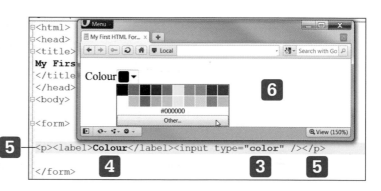

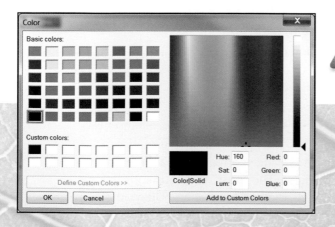

! ALERT: As with all other controls new to HTML5, browser support varies. Not all browsers will display the colour chooser the same way. Be sure to test cross-browser support before implementing the colour selector control (left).

Create a submit button

If you weren't aware, the `<button>` element isn't the only way to create a button. The `<input />` control can be used as a button too. Just set the type attribute value in an `<input />` tag to "submit" and the browser will display a submit button where the tag is. Set the value attribute to read whatever text you'd like on the button, and set the form's action and method to get the data submitted to a web server when the button is clicked.

1 Open the HTML form document in your text editor.

2 Add an `<input />` element to the `<form>` element.

3 Set the `<input />` element's type attribute to "submit".

4 Add a `<label>` element with text content 'Submit'.

5 Enclose both the `<input />` tag and `<label>` element within a `<p>` element.

6 Save the HTML document and open it in your web browser.

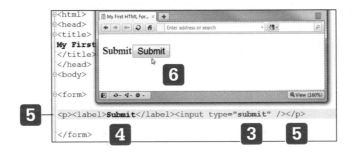

? DID YOU KNOW?
A submit button automatically knows where to send the data on the form based on the action and method attributes of the form.

? DID YOU KNOW?
The method and action attributes of a form provide information on where to submit form data, and the method for doing so. The "post" method sends the information as HTTP data, while the "get" method sends it as a URL-name value pair (which is far less secure).

Create a reset button

Just as the `<input />` tag can be set as a submit button, it can also be used as a reset button. The function of a reset button is very simple and clear: it clears all the data from the form. Set the type attribute of the `<input />` tag to "reset" to create a reset button.

1 Open the HTML form document in your text editor.

2 Add an `<input />` element to the `<form>` element.

3 Set the `<input />` element's type attribute to "reset".

4 Add a `<label>` element with text content 'Reset (will clear all data!)'.

5 Enclose both the `<input />` tag and `<label>` element within a `<p>` element.

6 Save the HTML document and open it in your web browser.

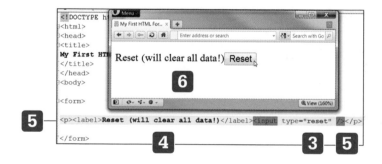

 HOT TIP: Be careful with reset buttons! User frustration can be very high if the button is not labelled clearly and all the form data is erased in one fell swoop with an accidental click. So, make sure the reset button is clearly labelled for its purpose!

Define an image as a button

The `<input />` tag can be set to use an image as a button. Set the type attribute to "image" to specify an image for use as a button. Custom user interfaces (UI) can be created using images to get the exact desired look and feel to the web page without loss of functionality.

1 Open the HTML form document in your text editor.

2 Add an `<input />` element to the `<form>` element.

3 Set the `<input />` element's type attribute to "image", the src attribute to the filename, and the alt to "btn".

4 Add a `<label>` element with text content 'Image button'.

5 Enclose both the `<input />` tag and `<label>` element within a `<p>` element.

6 Save the HTML document and open it in your web browser.

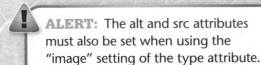

HOT TIP: Make sure the image chosen is the right size! The image will be used as is by the `<image />` tag, so make sure you have it sized correctly before adding it.

ALERT: The alt and src attributes must also be set when using the "image" setting of the type attribute.

HOT TIP: Be sure to use images which make clear the intent of the button, and be sure the users using your HTML form will be able to tell the image *is* a button!

8 Specifying CSS styles

Introduction

Cascading Style Sheets are text documents which contain instructions for browsers about how to display the elements of an HTML page. While HTML concerns itself largely with how a page is constructed, CSS concerns itself mostly with how a page appears. There are three different types of CSS style sheets: external, internal and inline.

External style sheets exist in a separate file from the HTML document they modify. An internal style sheet exists on the same sheet it modifies. And inline styles are applied to a single HTML element.

Each style sheet offers advantages and disadvantages, but the rules and usage are always the same. It's also possible to use inheritance – when one object or element gets properties or behaviours from a previously existing one – to combine styles and 'layer' their effect. An external style sheet and an internal style sheet may specify different rules about the same element and on that page the rules will be combined. Inline style sheets, however, allow specification of rules for a single element only, which eliminates some of the powerful selector tools CSS3 offers in external and `<style>` element sheets.

Find documentation on CSS

CSS3 information isn't hard to find. Nevertheless, a quick reference guide can be extremely helpful. It lists the CSS properties, their value settings, and also pseudo-classes, measurement units used in CSS and selectors with examples to choose any matching (or all) selectors. It's a very complete resource, and I highly recommend it. This task will guide you to one of the best ones I've found.

 Open http://www.w3.org/TR/#tr_CSS in your web browser.

 Bookmark the information about the CSS3 specification in your browser.

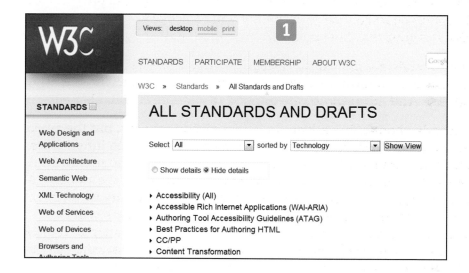

HOT TIP: You probably already have the W3C website bookmarked. If not, do so now: it can save you a lot of time searching the Internet later. You can find a lot of timely, helpful information there on CSS3 and HTML5, so it's one of your primary sources. Be sure to check the site out thoroughly, along with the WHATWG site at www.whatwg.org.

DID YOU KNOW?
Don't be too concerned if the terms like 'pseudo-classes' and 'selectors' don't seem to make much sense right now. They'll be covered in more detail as the book progresses and, where necessary, definitions will be provided.

3 Surf to http://veign.com/references/css3-guide.php in your web browser.

4 Download the CSS3 Quick Reference Guide if you haven't already done so.

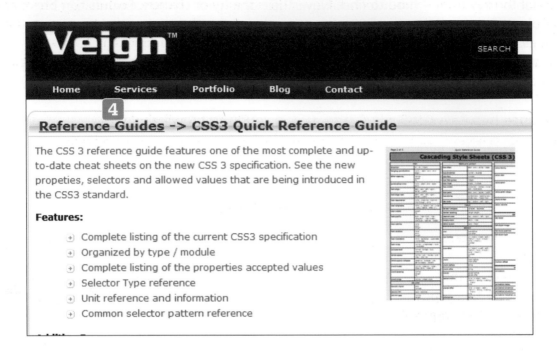

? DID YOU KNOW?

The W3C updates its website and the location of the specific document for CSS3's specification may change from time to time. Be sure to carefully examine the site when you visit to ensure you have the latest information about CSS3 and not an earlier version.

Find out what's new in CSS3

One of the key things about technology is the rapidity of change. Fortunately, there are people and organisations dedicated to keeping up with the change, and making sense of it all. They also present the information in helpful, easy-to-understand formats so anyone can check up on what's new and exciting in a single sitting and understand it without much trouble.

One such website is CSS3.info (http://css3.info). On it you will find terrific up-to-date information about CSS which will prove invaluable to you as a CSS developer.

1 Open your web browser and navigate to http://www.css3.info.

2 Click on the Module Status tab at the top of the screen.

3 Note the latest updates, and the status of all the modules being put through the approval process.

4 Bookmark the tab in your browser to return from time to time to check for new information or updates.

HOT TIP: Perusing information on a website may seem like a frivolous step around which to build an entire task, but it really isn't. It's a critical part of learning to properly use and understand CSS and its components. You can't effectively use something you don't know about, so bookmarking pages which tell you about what's new and ready is important.

DID YOU KNOW?

CSS3.info is one of the best blogs on the Internet for keeping track of what's happening with CSS3 and should be among the first, if not the first, stops you make when seeking CSS3-specific online information.

Prepare an HTML document for CSS

To save doing both HTML markup and CSS coding at the same time in each subsequent exercise, we'll make an HTML template we can use to save work. Save the template with a new name for each exercise to avoid overwriting the original file in case you need to revert to a clean copy. Our CSS coding will be done on the new copies. We'll use the template for the remainder of the book.

1 Open a new file in your text editor and save it with the name 'HTML_template.htm'.

2 Create an HTML DTD, html, title and body tags. Place the text 'CSS Template' inside the title element.

3 In the body element, add a header element and a footer element. Place 'This is the page header!' in the header element.

4 Between the header and footer elements, create a nav, an aside, a section and an article element.

5 In the nav element, add 'Link 1', 'Link 2' and 'Link 3' between the tags.

6 Save the HTML document.

```
<!DOCTYPE html>
<html>
<head>                    2
<title>CSS Template</title>
</head>
<body>                            3
<header>This is the page header!</header>
<nav>Link 1 Link 2 Link 3</nav>
<aside></aside>              5
<section></section>
<article></article>
<footer></footer>
</body>
</html>
```

 SEE ALSO: See 'Create a basic HTML document' in Chapter 2 for a primer on creating a basic HTML template structure.

 DID YOU KNOW?

CSS on its own won't be able to do anything. CSS requires an HTML page to format. While this task is about CSS, part of the prep work for the coming tasks in this and subsequent chapters requires we have something to apply CSS to, which is why we created this template.

? **DID YOU KNOW?**

The 'Lorem ipsum' generator will come in handy again as we create sample text to format for our CSS style sheets.

Understand CSS code

Like any language, CSS3 has parts and syntax which we must learn to make it work for us. CSS3 has declarations which format specific elements. The element selector chooses which element or elements will be formatted by the CSS declaration and is the first part of the declaration. On the same line beside the element is an open curly bracket ({), followed by the property declarations and the values for them. The rule is closed with a close curly bracket (}).

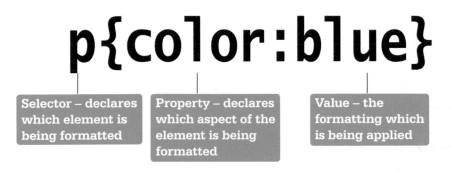

Selector – declares which element is being formatted

Property – declares which aspect of the element is being formatted

Value – the formatting which is being applied

Several kinds of formatting can be applied in a single declaration. Each property declaration is separated from its value by a colon, and a semi-colon separates properties inside the curly brackets.

It is also possible to use the same rule to format many elements. All the element selectors are listed before the curly brackets and separated by commas.

1. Navigate to http://www.freecsstemplates.org with your web browser.

2. Choose a CSS template from the selection and download it to your computer.

3. Open the newly downloaded index.html file in your browser to see how the page looks.

WHAT DOES THIS MEAN?

Syntax: the rules for appropriate use of components, whether computer or linguistic in nature, to form a cohesive language and grammatical structure. How components of a language of any kind are used to create the proper elements of the language.

4 Open the newly downloaded style.css file with your text editor and review the declarations.

5 Identify the selectors, properties and values in each declaration.

 DID YOU KNOW?
Cascading style sheets usually contain multiple declarations unless they're inline styles applied to a single element.

 DID YOU KNOW?
External style sheets can declare all the formatting for a site in a single location.

 DID YOU KNOW?
Style sheets, particularly external ones, can be quite lengthy. Most websites use intricate style sheets to control formatting and provide a uniform appearance to the site. To facilitate ease of code interpretation, declarations are often broken out line-by-line rather than made over a single line. Don't be confused by CSS declarations laid out this way. HTML can be written with various indent schemes to clarify code also. The layout has no impact whatsoever on the way CSS works.

Create CSS comments

To annotate CSS code, use CSS comments. They work the same as comments in other programming or markup languages – they are not displayed or interpreted by the browser at all, but are visible behind the scenes.

Comments are used to explain code, make notes, and as reminders to the programmer for various tasks. CSS comment starting markers are a forward slash and an asterisk (/*) while the closing marker is a mirror image (*/).

1 Open the style.css file from your downloaded CSS template using your text editor.

2 Locate the first comment in the file.

3 Identify the start indicator (/*) and the closing indicator (*/).

4 Note the other CSS comments annotating the rest of the style.css file.

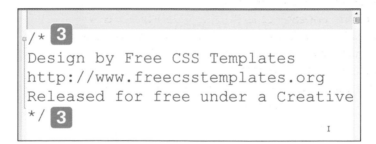

```
/* 3
Design by Free CSS Templates
http://www.freecsstemplates.org
Released for free under a Creative
*/ 3
                                    I
```

? DID YOU KNOW?

If you use Notepad++ or a similar text editor, comments for all code are indicated by coloured text. In Notepad++ the default is green. This is a helpful feature for reading code.

▶ SEE ALSO: See the 'Understand CSS code' section of this chapter for instructions on downloading a CSS template from the web.

Understand classes and ids

Elements can be selected by class or id (identifier) to format, and formatting applied only to those specific elements, by using HTML class and id attributes.

The id attribute makes a single element unique so it can have formatting applied just to that element. A class makes a group of elements unique. Formatting can be applied to a class so all members of the class are formatted at once. In this way some elements of a certain type (like paragraphs, for instance) can be formatted while others aren't.

1 Open the index.htm file from your downloaded CSS template in your text editor.

2 Find any '#' (hash mark) characters in the file.

3 Note the formatting applied to those declarations. These are specific identifiers.

```
#wrapper {
    width: 980px;
    margin: 0 auto;
    padding: 0;
}

/* Header */
2
#header {
    width: 980px;
    height: 280px;    3
    margin: 0 auto;
    padding: 0px;
    background: url(images/img06.g
}
```

 HOT TIP: An id for an element is analogous to a name. You can create rules for individual elements among the other elements and class elements by specifying the name in the rule(s).

 DID YOU KNOW?
The need for the <div> element is diminished in HTML5 because specific structural elements such as the <aside>, <section> and <article> elements provide better page structure.

Those familiar with object-orient (OO) programming principles won't have trouble understanding HTML classes. But for those who aren't OO programmers, think about automobiles as an example. An automobile, in our example, is an object. A van is a class of automobile (or object). It shares many features with the automobile object but has its own unique qualities which make it slightly different. Setting the class attribute for an HTML element or group of elements creates a unique class which can be addressed apart from all other similar elements. In our automobile example, it is possible to make all vans blue without affecting any other class of car. Individual classes can be formatted apart from all other classes. One class of paragraph elements can be formatted without affecting other paragraphs by creating CSS rules for the class and adding the desired paragraph elements to the class by setting the class id.

DID YOU KNOW?

Generic `<div>` elements are created as 'wrappers' for content which can have CSS formatting applied to them. This element was introduced in an earlier version of HTML and is still in use; CSS3 is able to format those generic division structures.

DID YOU KNOW?

Classes simply group HTML elements together. Specific element property formatting can then be applied only to the elements of the class.

Create an external style sheet

External style sheets are text documents with all the formatting CSS rules on them. They are saved with a .css extension. Websites link to the external style sheets through the `<link />` tag, which is placed in the `<head>` element of the HTML file. The website then retrieves the rules for each of the selectors in the CSS document and applies them to all the pages of a website which are linked to the CSS file.

1 Open a new document in your text editor and save it in the same folder with your HTML template as 'style.css'.

2 On the first line of the style sheet, type the letter 'p' followed by a space, then a curly bracket, like this: p {

3 Inside the curly bracket, type: color:blue. (Note the US spelling of 'color'!)

```
1  p {color:blue;}

   2      3      4
```

4 Type a semi-colon, a closing curly bracket, save the file and close it.

5 Notice the file isn't linked to an HTML document yet and does nothing.

The `<link>` element defines the relationship of the linked resource to the current page. The href attribute is set to the URL of the style sheet on the web server, and all the rules of relative and absolute URL linking apply. It works exactly the same as the href attribute for the `<a>` tag. The `<link>` tag is an empty tag.

The `<link />` tag may have the type attribute in it, which lists the type of style sheet the browser should expect. The browser can then ignore any unsupported style sheets in favour of those it does support.

HOT TIP: Using an external style sheet has the distinct advantage of ease of maintenance. Changing the look of an entire site can be done from a single location rather than having to alter each individual page, or each element of a particular type throughout a website. A single change can have broad-reaching impact. Entire sites can get a new look and feel with a few simple lines of code added or edited in the .css file.

? DID YOU KNOW?

The designer must be careful in using internal or inline styles alongside external style sheets. Because they are the highest level of formatting instruction, all lower levels are either added to their rules or override them altogether. Depending upon placement in the `<head>` element, internal style sheets might supplant an external style sheet inadvertently. Inheritance can create strange or undesirable effects. If a certain page requires a specific appearance, it may be easier to create a lower-level layer of formatting if the page does not change frequently.

Link an HTML file to an external style sheet

To use an external style sheet to format an HTML page, the two must be linked through the HTML file's `<link />` tag. Set the `<link />` tag's href attribute to the location and file name of the style sheet. Set the rel attribute to "stylesheet" for their relationship. If you do not link the CSS to the HTML document the formatting will not be applied. The `<link />` tag is an open element and has no closing tag.

1 Open the HTML template with your text editor and save it with a new name.

2 In the `<head>` section, create a `<link />` tag.

3 Set the rel attribute to "style sheet" and the href attribute to the location of the style sheet to link to.

4 Add 'Lorem ipsum' text enclosed in `<p>` elements to the `<section>` and `<article>` elements.

5 Save the HTML template.

6 Open it in your web browser to see the formatting applied to the HTML file.

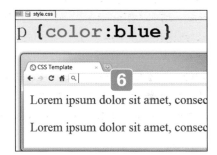

ALERT: Spelling counts! If you misspell or leave off any punctuation from the attribute or markup at all, you will probably not see the expected results.

HOT TIP: If the CSS and HTML files are in the same folder location, you only need the file name in the href attribute to link the two correctly.

HOT TIP: Use the copy and paste feature of your text editor to make sure you accurately capture the location of the style sheet for the `<link />` tag's href attribute.

Create an internal style sheet

The only differences between internal style sheets and external ones are where they are placed and how many documents are formatted. The `<style>` element is added to the `<head>` element with the CSS rules between the tags. This formats only the page where it resides.

The `<style>` element has the type attribute which is identical to the type attribute of the `<link />` tag. For our purposes the value is "text/css". There is, however, no need for an href or rel attribute, since the style sheet exists directly on the web page it formats.

1 Open your HTML template with your text editor and save it with a new name.

2 In the `<head>` element, add the `<style>` element.

3 In the style element's start tag, add the type attribute with the value "text/css".

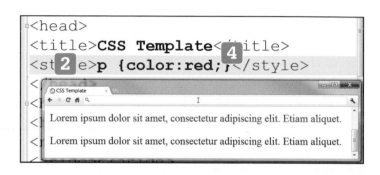

4 Create a CSS rule between the tags to make the `<p>` element content red:
p {color:red;}

? DID YOU KNOW?

We are only changing font colour now to see the results of our style sheets. More elaborate formatting will be done in subsequent chapters. This chapter's tasks are only to familiarise you with creating style sheets.

HOT TIP: When used together, the position of the `<style>` element and the `<link>` element is critical. If the position is reversed the external style sheet may override the effects of the internal style sheet.

HOT TIP: After the declaration of the style sheet, the syntax for all the rules remains the same. You don't need to learn a new way of coding CSS for an internal style sheet.

Create an inline style sheet

Inline style sheets are created inside the start tag of a specific element to format. They are the 'last resort' of formatting and so they override conflicting formatting rules in either internal or external style sheets.

Inline styles are declared with the style attribute of the element. The attribute value applies the formatting. They follow the same general syntax as the external and internal style sheets, but the curly brackets aren't required within the style attribute. Remember to enclose all HTML attribute values in double quotes!

1 Open your HTML template in your text editor and save it with a new name.

2 Create a `<p>` element in the `<section>` element with 'Lorem ipsum' text as content.

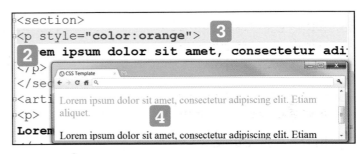

3 In the `<p>` start tag, add the style attribute and set the value to turn the paragraph text orange: "color:orange"

4 Save the HTML file and open it in a web browser to view the results.

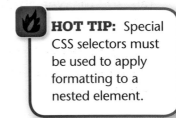

HOT TIP: Special CSS selectors must be used to apply formatting to a nested element.

? DID YOU KNOW?

Inheritance in CSS means that rules which are not specified in one style sheet but are specified in another are passed to the formatted element anyway. For instance, if you change the font face in the external style sheet and the font colour in an internal style sheet for the same element, both formatting levels are applied. In this way, it is possible to have a particular element inherit formatting from all three levels of style sheets.

? DID YOU KNOW?

In previous versions of HTML, a `<span>` or `<div>` element could be used to group certain elements together. With HTML5's much more specific structural elements, grouping with the `<span>` and `<div>` elements isn't as necessary any more. Specific styles, however, can still be applied to grouped elements using the `<span>` and `<div>` elements as wrappers for formatting.

Use simple CSS selectors

A CSS3 selector is the portion of CSS code which chooses the element or group of elements to apply formatting to. A simple selector chooses only one type of element. All the elements of that type will have the formatting applied to them.

1 Open your HTML document with your text editor.

2 Add a `<p>` element to the `<body>` element. Your 'Lorem ipsum' text may be useful here.

3 Create a new file in your text editor and call it 'style.css'.

4 Add a declaration for a `<p>` element which changes the text to blue: p {color:blue;}

5 Add a `<link />` tag in the `<head>` tag and set the href value to the style sheet you just created.

6 Save the CSS file, save the HTML file with a new name, and open it with your web browser.

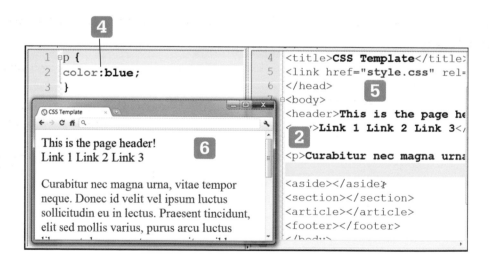

▶ **SEE ALSO:** Some of the formatting used for demonstration purposes here will be covered in more detail later in the book.

? **DID YOU KNOW?**

Selectors in CSS can be combined to specifically choose particular elements. Those combinations are called 'combinators' and are very powerful tools for web design.

Use CSS class selectors

CSS3 allows selection of elements to format by class instead of types. For instance, rather than choosing all paragraph elements, you can create an HTML class of paragraph called 'special' and apply formatting just to those paragraphs in the class. Specific classes are chosen using the simple selector, a full stop or 'dot', and then the property and value: p.special {*property: value;*}

1 Open your HTML document with your text editor.

2 Add two `<p>` with content to the `<body>` element, one with a class of "green":
`<p class="green"></p>`

3 Create a new file in your text editor and call it 'style.css'.

4 Add a declaration for the `<p class="green">` element to change the text to green: p.green {color:green;}

5 Add a `<link />` tag in the `<head>` tag and set the href value to the style sheet you just created.

6 Save the CSS file, save the HTML file with a new name, and open it with your web browser.

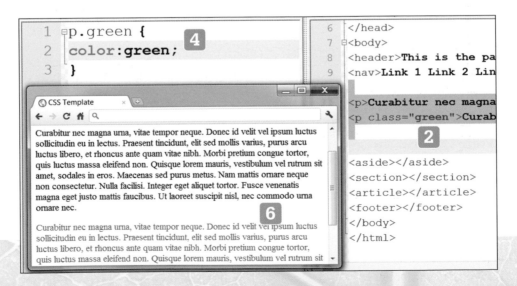

 HOT TIP: Using classes is a very efficient and powerful way to have different formatting applied to the same types of elements, such as paragraphs or headings.

 ALERT: Be aware, *only* the elements of the selected class will have the formatting applied!

Use CSS id selectors

HTML elements can be given identifiers, or ids, which make them unique. CSS3 uses those identifiers to pick out a single element from a type or class and apply formatting only to the specified element. Identifier selectors use the type, followed by a hash symbol (#), and then the identifier as found in the id attribute of the element to be formatted.

1 Open your HTML document with your text editor.

2 Add two `<p>` with content to the `<body>` element, one with an id of "fmt": `<p id="fmt"></p>`

3 Create a new file in your text editor and call it 'style. css'.

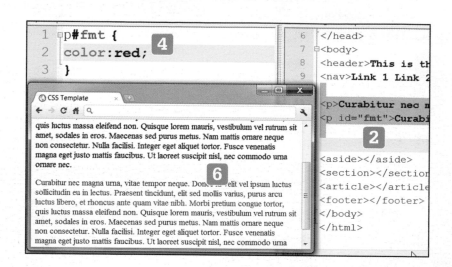

4 Add a declaration for the `<p id-"fmt">` element to change the text to red: p#fmt {color:red;}

5 Add a `<link />` tag in the `<head>` tag and set the href value to the style sheet you just created.

6 Save the CSS file, save the HTML file with a new name, and open it with your web browser.

? DID YOU KNOW?

If the type is left off the selector, any element with the id selector specified in the declaration will have the formatting applied, regardless of type. You can therefore have the same formatting applied to very different types of elements as long as they share the same id attribute value.

🔥 HOT TIP: If a single element has more than one identifier attribute, they must all be specified for the formatting to work.

9 Setting borders and colours with CSS

Introduction

CSS provides formatting options for almost everything on a web page. This includes choosing colours and styles for things on the web page. Since almost everything on a web page has a border around it, and since almost all elements of HTML can have colours applied, CSS offers several ways to format colours, including by hexadecimal value, by RGB percentage or value, or by colour name.

CSS3 offers exciting new options for borders, such as rounded element corners, which previously could only be obtained using images created in graphics programs such as Adobe Photoshop®.

CSS3 allows colours and borders to be added to specific elements using new selectors and combinators which make web design easier and more powerful than ever before.

Combinators are CSS code operators which are placed between simple selectors to allow granular selection of elements on a web page for formatting. A simple selector is the portion of a CSS rule which selects the element to be formatted. Simple selectors select only one element at a time without targeting parent or child elements.

Add a border to an element

Borders are the outline of an element's shape, composed of lines, and with CSS the lines can be formatted. They can be made dotted lines, dashed lines, solid lines, combinations of dots and dashes, and even images can be used as borders.

It's also possible to control individual parts of a border so one section of the border differs from the others. Control of element borders can be the difference between an exciting page for the eye and a boring one.

1 Open the HTML template with your text editor and save it with a new name.

2 Add an `<h1>` element to the top of the body section with the content 'This is the page header!'.

3 Add a `<link />` tag to your HTML file with href set to "style.css" and rel set to "stylesheet", then save the file.

4 Create a style.css file with your text editor in the same location as the HTML document from step 1.

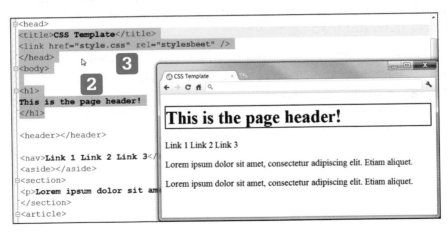

 HOT TIP: Adding borders is simple, and offers the eye a ready and easily recognisable divider between portions of HTML pages, such as sections, articles or headings and footers.

? DID YOU KNOW?

The `<h1>` declaration you created in the CSS file will format all `<h1>` elements you add to the page, but you will have to specify `<h1>` elements which reside inside other elements. This is what combinators are used for in CSS.

5 Add a declaration for h1 elements as follows: h1 {border:2px solid black;}

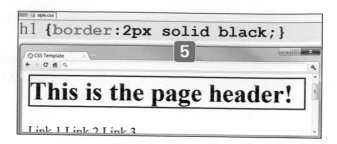

6 Save the style.css file then refresh the sample web page in your browser to view the results.

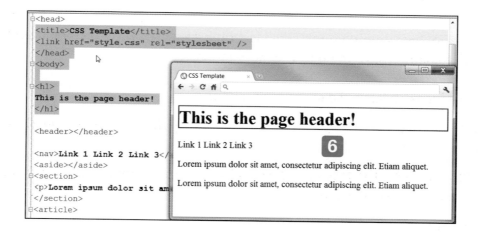

? **DID YOU KNOW?**

The h1 declaration created for this exercise formats the border of the h1 element to be a solid, black line of 2 pixels thickness. Refer to the documentation you have for CSS3 for details on the properties for borders.

▶ **SEE ALSO:** For more information on using images as borders, please see *Brilliant HTML5 & CSS3* by Josh Hill and James A. Brannen (2011, Pearson Education).

Create borders using separate lines

Line colour, style and width can be set for each line in a border independently. Rather than a single border property, each of the properties is set with its own CSS declaration.

```
h1 {
border-left-color: black;
border-right-color: blue;
border-bottom-style: dotted;
border-top-width: 5px;
}
```

Each declaration ends with a semi-colon and the properties are separated from their values with a colon, just as in other CSS declarations.

1 Create a blank style.css file in your text editor.

2 Create a declaration for the `<header>` element to place a border around the page header.

3 Add properties for the top, right and left borders to be solid black lines 1px thick, with the bottom border 5px.

4 Save the style.css file but don't close it.

5 Open the HTML template in your text editor and save with a new name.

6 Add the `<link />` tag to your newly created style.css file, then save and close both documents.

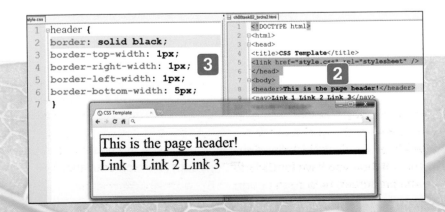

Create rounded corners on a border

CSS3 can create rounded corners for borders without using images made in software like Adobe Photoshop®. The property for doing this is border-radius when all four corners will receive the same radius. The radius value is expressed as pixels. The corners can be rounded individually as well using the following properties:

```
border-top-right-radius
border-bottom-right-radius
border-top-left-radius
border-bottom-left-radius
```

1 Create a blank style.css file with your text editor.

2 Open the HTML template and save it with a new name.

3 Add a declaration in style.css to place borders around the `<header>` section (use the code from the 'Create borders using separate lines' section in this chapter).

4 Apply a corner radius of 12px to all four corners of the borders (see the code in the screenshot).

5 Add the `<link />` tag to your `<head>` section in the HIML file with href set to your style.css file.

6 Save both files and open the HTML document in the browser.

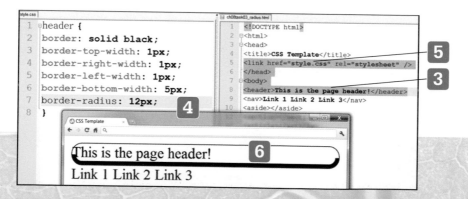

HOT TIP: Using the border-radius property is simple and easily visible, as the results of this task show, and can add a nice dimension to web page design.

Choose a colour palette

CSS colours are specified using RGB, hexadecimal or name values. Sixteen-bit capability provides 65,536 colour choices while 32 bits provides 16,777,216 colour choices.

There are two important design considerations when choosing your site's colours. First, the ability to use thousands of colours doesn't forgo strong aesthetics. Second, many monitors for various reasons do not display colours accurately in all cases, and so may not display subtle colour differences correctly.

1 Open your web browser.

2 Navigate to the Color Schemer Online colour palette tool at www.colorschemer. com/online.html.

3 Enter #B22222 (firebrick) as the hexadecimal value and click the Set HEX button.

4 Now navigate to www.december.com with your web browser.

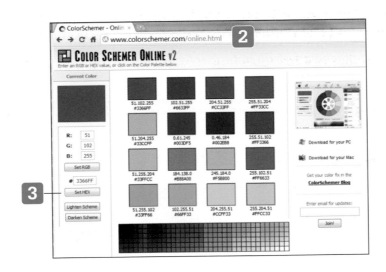

? DID YOU KNOW?

Some colours look good together and others don't. You might spend hours choosing a subtle, artistic colour combination that doesn't display well for all users. Aim for contrast rather than subtle colour differences. Contrast does not mean your sight must be garish, however. Be sure to stay within the palate selected. Note the set of complementary colours produce a pleasing appearance for a website.

5 From the home page, click on 'Hex Hub!' in the 'Encounter' box.

6 Select a pre-defined palette in the warm or cool range, or neutrals and blacks.

7 Notice the site provides the hexadecimal number and the name value for the colours in the table shown.

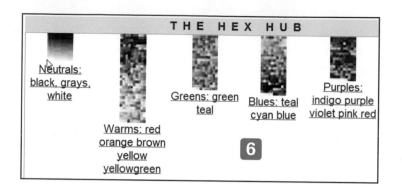

HOT TIP: When using a desktop palette selection tool, remember subtle colour differences may not render well on some users' monitors. Go for more rather than less colour contrast.

Specify CSS colour by name

In order to change the default colour for any element on a web page, you must specify a different colour for the browser to apply. It can be almost any colour – as discussed earlier, the number of colour choices available soars into the millions – but you must pick one.

There are four ways to specify CSS colours. The first is to use the colour's name.

```
color: cornflowerblue;
```

1 Create a blank style.css file using your text editor.

2 Add a declaration for the `<header>` element which turns the text blue: header {color: blue;}

3 Save the CSS file and close it.

4 Open the HTML template and save it with a new name.

5 Add the `<link />` tag with the href property set to the location and name of the style.css file you just created.

6 Open the newly saved HTML document in your web browser.

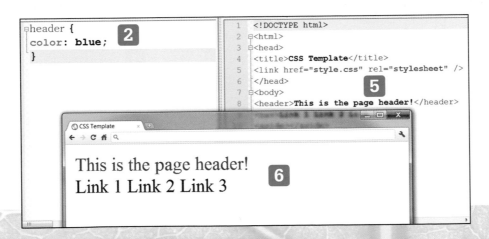

? **DID YOU KNOW?**

The property used in this task, color, is the foreground colour of the selected element. The background colour is selected separately and is covered later in this chapter.

Specify CSS colour by hexadecimal value

Hexadecimal values are frequently used to determine colours digitally. Many photography and illustration programs such as Adobe Photoshop® provide hexadecimal values for colours to precisely control colour choices. CSS3 can also use hexadecimal (or 'hex') values to specify colours in property declaration, like this: `color: #6495ED` Note the hash mark before the colour value – it's critical and the colour will not show without it.

1 Create a blank style.css file with your text editor.

2 Add a declaration for the `<heading>` element on the first line.

3 In the declaration rules, specify a violet-blue with the colour value: color: 1111ee;

4 Add the `<link />` tag in the HTML document `<head>` section with href set to the style.css file you just created.

5 Save the HTML document.

6 Open it in your web browser.

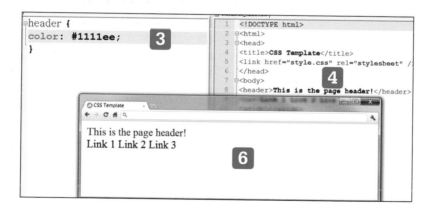

```
header {
  color: #1111ee;        3
}
```

```
1   <!DOCTYPE html>
2   <html>
3   <head>
4   <title>CSS Template</title>
5   <link href="style.css" rel="stylesheet" /
6   </head>
7   <body>
8   <header>This is the page header!</header>
```
4

CSS Template

This is the page header!
Link 1 Link 2 Link 3

6

ALERT: Don't confuse the `<head>` element with the `<heading>` element! Both are structural elements, but the `<head>` element contains information about the HTML document and isn't visible. The `<heading>` element groups content in a heading.

HOT TIP: Hexadecimal values aren't case-sensitive. 1111ee is the same colour as 1111EE.

Specify CSS colour by RGB percentage

RGB stands for Red, Green, Blue and it signifies the amount of those colours added to the final, onscreen colour selected. The use of RGB percentages in CSS dictates what levels of red, blue and green will be included in the colour you're setting. While it's not used very often, it is available as an option, for example: `color: rgb(39%, 58%, 93%);`

1 Create a blank style.css file with your text editor.

2 Add a declaration for the `<heading>` element on the first line.

3 In the declaration rules, specify a mossy-green colour as follows:
   `color: rgb(33%, 55%, 12%);`

4 Add the `<link />` tag in the HTML document `<head>` section with href set to the style.css file you just created.

5 Save the HTML document.

6 Open it in your web browser.

ALERT: Notice this method of specifying colour doesn't require the hash mark in front of the colour declaration value. Putting it in makes the declaration fail.

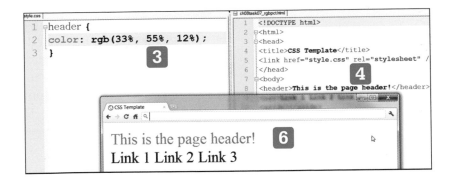

 HOT TIP: Play with the percentages in the declaration so you can watch how the colour changes with each save and reload. This method of colour specification provides more control than simply naming a colour to use.

Specify CSS colour by RGB values

The RGB value signifies the amounts of red, green and blue in the colour. This specifies the precise mix of each part of the colour to define what appears on screen, for example: `color: rgb(100,149,237);`

1 Create a blank style.css file with your text editor.

2 Add a declaration for the `<heading>` element on the first line.

3 In the declaration rules, specify a reddish colour as follows: color: rgb(225,12,18);

4 Add the `<link />` tag in the HTML document `<head>` section with the href set to the style.css file you just created.

5 Save the HTML document.

6 Open it in your web browser.

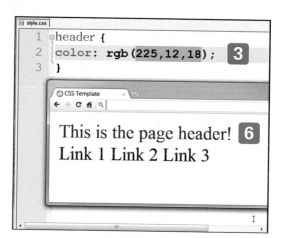

 HOT TIP: Copy and paste is your friend! Where multiple rules which are identical are to be created and where a single declaration cannot be made for them, don't hesitate to copy and paste your properties from one rule to another to save typing.

ALERT: Beware! The colour values for RGB declaration are limited to whole numbers (no decimals) between 0 and 255 only.

Set foreground colours

Declaring a foreground colour for an element with CSS is simple. The element's colour is declared in a rule. Nothing else to it; just declare the colour. For example:

```
body {color: lime;}
```

In general, the foreground of an element is the text content. The `color` property therefore applies to text for the most part. This includes formatting HTML tags like `<em>`, `<strong>` and `<sup>`.

```
strong {color: red;}
em {color: #E3372E;}
```

Any element can have a colour declared; however, setting the colour for an element without text content (like a horizontal rule) has no effect. Remember this rule of thumb: no text, no foreground colour.

1 Create a style.css file in your text editor.

2 Add a CSS declaration which sets the header element's foreground to the value 'gray': `color: gray;`

3 Save the style sheet file.

4 Open the HTML template and save it with a new name.

5 Add the `<link />` element to the `<head>` section with the href value set to the style.css file you just created.

6 Save the HTML document and open it in your text editor.

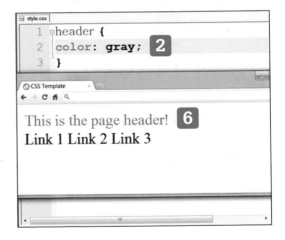

```
style.css
  1  header {
  2  color: gray;   2
  3  }
```

CSS Template

This is the page header!   6
Link 1 Link 2 Link 3

DID YOU KNOW?
The colour for a single element or particular text can be overridden by setting the text colour for a paragraph element or by using an inline style sheet.

Set background colours

Any element can have a background colour. CSS makes background colours possible through the background-color declaration. The declared colour is displayed as the background colour of the element selected in CSS.

It's normal practice to vary background colours in different parts of a web page to offer clarity of view, legibility or to draw attention. Most web pages do not have much more than simple black-on-white or black-on-grey schemes for text content, but occasionally a white-on-black or white-on-grey page will be used, particularly for personal websites and blogs. The bright text against a dark background is a bit harder on the eyes for most viewers, so this scheme is used less frequently in professional websites.

1 Create a style.css file in your text editor.

2 Add a CSS declaration to set the body element's background to grey: background-color: gray;

3 Save the style sheet file.

4 Open the HTML template and save it with a new name.

5 Add the `<link />` element to the `<head>` section with the href value set to the style.css file you just created.

6 Save the HTML document and open it in your text editor.

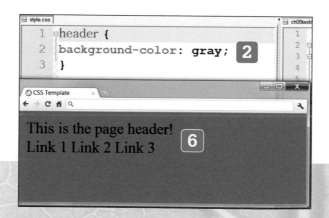

HOT TIP: Note the US spellings for all CSS declarations. Using UK spellings won't work!

Set background images

Any element can have an image as its background using the CSS background-image property. For example:

```
body {background-image: url(./myimage.png);}
```

The image chosen will be repeated across the screen according to the properties set in the CSS rule. Our formatted sample web page isn't conducive to the image used for the task examples, but it gives you an idea of what can be done with images and backgrounds.

 HOT TIP: Consult your Quick Reference Guide downloaded from www.veign.com for more background code snippets to set backgrounds.

1 Select an image to use for a background – either download one (legally!) or use one from your own stock.

2 Create a new style.css file in your text editor.

3 Add a declaration to set the image as the body element background: body {background-image: url(chrysanthemum.jpg);}

4 Save the CSS file, then open your HTML template and save it with a new name.

5 Add a `<link />` tag to the `<head>` element and set the href value to the style.css file you just created.

6 Save the HTML file and open it in your web browser.

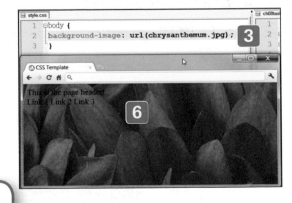

 HOT TIP: Don't let the use of the 'url' portion of the CSS declaration fool you. The URL location can be a file on your local computer. Using relative or absolute URLs will work. For the purposes of this exercise, saving the image you will use as your background to the same location as the HTML and CSS files means you can simply use the file name in the URL value.

 DID YOU KNOW?
If your image is smaller than the web page dimensions, the image used for the background will automatically repeat to fill the entire background. This is called 'tiling'.

Tile background images horizontally

It may be useful to have a single image repeat across a page, such as when creating gradient backgrounds. A background image can be tiled horizontally across the page to create such an effect with CSS3's background-repeat property declaration:

```
background-repeat: repeat-x;
```

The 'x' represents the horizontal axis of an x–y axis grid. This tells the browser to repeat the image horizontally across the page.

1 Create a new style.css file in your text editor.

2 Create a declaration to set an image as the background for the `<body>` element.

3 In the `<body>` element declaration, add a rule to set the background to repeat:
```
background-repeat: repeat-x;
```

4 Save the style.css file and close it.

5 Open your HTML template with your text editor and save it with a new name.

6 Add a `<link />` tag with the href attribute set to the newly created style.css file.

7 Save the HTML file and open it in your web browser.

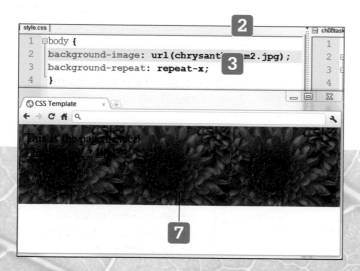

HOT TIP: Be careful when you choose an image to use for a background. If the colours are too strong or the image is too busy, it will detract from, not enhance, your web page!

▶ **SEE ALSO:** See the 'Set background images' section in this chapter for details on using an image as the background for an element.

Tile background images vertically

Just as an image can be tiled across the page, it can also be tiled down the page. The background image can be tiled vertically with the CSS background-repeat property, set to the value of `repeat-y`:

```
background-repeat: repeat-y;
```

The 'y' portion of the declaration denotes the y-axis of an x–y axis, which will repeat the image vertically on the page.

1 Create a blank style.css file and add a declaration to set a background image for the `<body>` element.

2 In the declaration add a rule to repeat the image vertically on the page:
`background-repeat: repeat-y;`

3 Save and close the CSS file.

4 Open your HTML template and save it with a new name.

5 Add a `<link />` tag with the href attribute set to your new style.css file.

6 Save the HTML document and open the HTML document in your web browser.

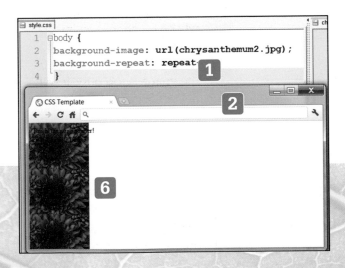

HOT TIP: Use images which aren't too powerful, bright and busy for background images. Otherwise the content will be lost and the page will look amateurish.

SEE ALSO: See the 'Set background images' section earlier in this chapter for more information on using background images.

Position background images with CSS

Images can be positioned on a page using CSS3. To centre the picture on the page, the background-position declaration is used, with the desired position of the image as the value setting:

```
background-position: top center;
```

Other settings include top left, top right, bottom left, bottom center (note the US spelling) and bottom right.

1 Create a blank style.css file with your text editor.

2 Add a declaration to set an image as the background for the body element, with *no repeat*.

3 Add a declaration to position the image on the page as follows: background-position: top center;

4 Save and close the style.css file.

5 Open the HTML template in your text editor.

6 Add a <link /> tag with the href attribute set to the style.css file you created.

7 Save the HTML document with a new name and open it in your web browser.

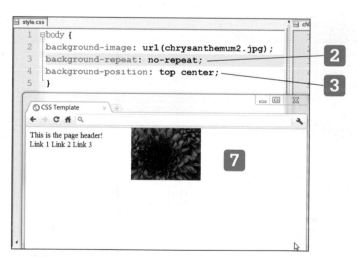

SEE ALSO: See the 'Set background images' section earlier in this chapter for details on setting a background image with CSS3.

10 Formatting fonts and text with CSS

Introduction

HTML provides some measure of formatting ability, but CSS is the preferred way of handling formatting in web pages. There are other formatting choices available also, many of which were impossible in HTML attributes. There are CSS properties to underline, overline, strikethrough, change case, and cause text to flash or blink, and for text alignment and spacing. Any HTML text can be properly formatted using CSS text and font properties so your web designs are unified and pleasing.

Because CSS is much more powerful and provides many options unavailable with HTML formatting tags, the formatting done by HTML has largely been deprecated or phased out. Use CSS properties to ensure the browser will display the formatting properly, since support for deprecated formatting cannot be ensured across all versions of all browsers.

Set an element's font-family

A font-family is a set of similarly designed fonts and generic font-families are common to all browsers. They're the safest choice to ensure the specified font is available and are declared with the font-family property.

With the font-family declaration, multiple fonts can be listed, separated by commas, to ensure a user's system has the one needed. It's good practice to end the list with one of the five generic font-family values such as serif or sans-serif. The browser then displays whichever one matches the system font available. For example:

```
p {font-family: arial, tahoma, serif;}
```

1 Create a style.css file with your text editor with a font-family declaration as follows: `font-family: tahoma, arial, sans-serif;`

2 Save the style sheet and close it.

3 Open the HTML template in your text editor.

4 Add text content in your `<body>` element.

5 Add the `<link />` tag to the `<head>` element with the href attribute set to the newly created style.css file.

6 Save and launch the HTML document in your web browser.

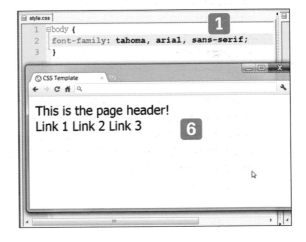

 DID YOU KNOW?

Not all fonts exist on all computer systems. To use an uncommon font, create the text as you'd like it to look and turn it into a PNG image with a transparent background with any photo-editing software such as Adobe Photoshop®.

HOT TIP: When using font-family, if the font's name has white space in it, enclose the font-family value in single or double quotations, for example: `p{font-family: "DejaVu Sans";}`

Set an element's font-style

Font-styles are how a font is rendered. There are three standard styles: normal, italic or oblique. Many fonts also have bold and bold italic styles. The font-style is declared with the font-style property. Not all fonts have the same styles, and not all systems have all styles for all fonts. This means a browser may not be able to format in the expected way for every visitor. All fonts have a normal style, which is the default if the font-style declaration is omitted.

1 Create a new style.css file with your text editor.

2 Add a declaration for the `<body>` element to set the font style to italics: `font-style: italic;`

3 Save the style.css file and close it.

4 Open the HTML template in the text editor.

This is the page header!
Link 1 Link 2 Link 3

5 Add the `<link />` tag with the href set to the style.css file just created.

6 Save the HTML document with a new name and open it in your web browser.

▶ **SEE ALSO:** Remember, many HTML tags change the appearance of text. In many situations these tags are more appropriate than specifying a font. See Chapter 3, 'Using HTML text markup tags', for more information on HTML text formatting tags.

❓ **DID YOU KNOW?**
There are three other font properties not covered here. The font-size-adjust property allows adjusting a font's size, while font-stretch allows stretching or condensing a font. The font-variant property allows setting a font's variant. But there are only two variants, normal and small-caps. For more information on these properties, see the W3C's website (www.w3.org).

❓ **DID YOU KNOW?**
Italicised fonts are independent fonts from their normal style counterparts and may have special designs for certain characters which differ from the normal style. Arial Italics, for example, is an independent system font. When a browser is instructed to load Arial Italics it loads the Arial Italics system font rather than 'italicising' the Arial font. In contrast, the oblique value may simply display the font at a slant, though not necessarily.

Set font-weight

Font-weight means how thickly, or heavily, a font's lines are drawn by the browser. Bold fonts use heavier lines than normal fonts. In CSS, the font-weight property takes the values normal, bold, bolder, lighter, or 100, 200, 300, 400, 500, 600, 700, 800 and 900. The default is normal. So, for example:

```
p {font-weight: bolder;}
p.big1 {font-weight: 900;}
p.big2 {font-weight: 500%;}
```

1 Create a new style.css file in your text editor.

2 Add a declaration to make the `<body>` element font weight bold: `font-weight: bold;`

3 Save the style sheet and close it.

4 Open your HTML element with your text editor.

5 Add a `<link />` tag to the `<head>` element with the href set to the style. css file you just created.

6 Save the HTML file and open it in your web browser.

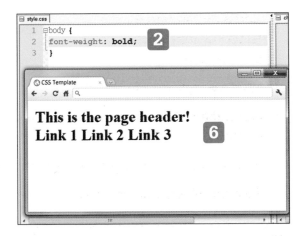

 DID YOU KNOW?

A font's weight is inherited from its parent element. That is, setting an element's font-weight to bold causes any elements nested inside it to have bold text also applied.

 DID YOU KNOW?

The values bolder and lighter are relative to the parent element's font. The browser increases the font's weight relative to the parent element font.

DID YOU KNOW?

Specifying by percentage sets the font-weight relative to its parent: 500% means five times the font-weight of the parent element font.

Set font-size

Font-size is how large the actual individual characters are rendered by the browser. Font-size is declared with the font-size property. Valid values are: xx-small, x-small, small, medium, large, x-large, larger, smaller, a percentage, or length. The first six values (xx-small to x-large) are absolute values, as is setting a length. The larger, smaller and percentage values are relative to the parent's font-size. The relative length units are em, ex and px. For example:

```
p {font-size:16px;}
h1{font-size:2em;}
```

1 Create a blank style.css file in your text editor.

2 Add a declaration to set the `<body>` element font-size to xx-large: `font-size: xx-large;`

3 Save and close the CSS file.

4 Open the HTML template with your text editor.

5 Add a `<link />` element with href set to the newly created style.css file.

6 Save the HTML file with a new name and open it in your web browser.

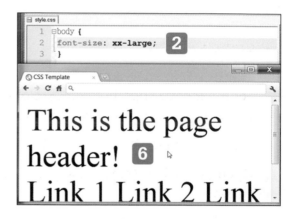

 **DID YOU KNOW?**

It may be difficult to see the difference in font-size initially. Add a declaration to set the font-size of a different element on the HTML template to x-small (font-size: x-small;) or xx-small to make it more obvious.

DID YOU KNOW?

Relative font-size means relative to the font-size of whatever the parent element is. When the property is applied to the `<body>` element, all the elements within the `<body>` will receive that font size.

Set font properties with the font declaration

A font's CSS properties don't need to be set singularly with separate declarations. CSS provides a single font declaration which sets multiple font properties at once, such as the font-style, font-weight, font-size and font-family. For example:

```
p {font: normal bold 12pt Times, serif;}
```

The benefits of using a single font declaration are space saving in the CSS file, readability and efficiency. Doing more with less code is always a plus.

 Create a new style.css file in your text editor and add a font declaration for the `<header>` element.

 Set the font to 30pt, bold font-weight and Arial font or font-family values: `font: bold 30pt Arial, sans-serif;`

3 Save the style.css file and close it.

4 Open your HTML template in your text editor.

5 Add the `<link />` tag to the `<head>` element with the href value set to the newly created style.css file.

6 Save the HTML file with a new name and open it in your web browser.

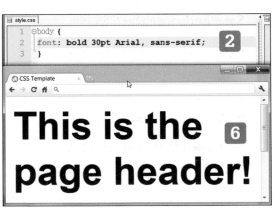

? DID YOU KNOW?
It may not be possible to set all font properties with a single declaration in all instances. While using the convenient 'all-in-one' declarations offers efficiency, it may not be possible to do everything required with it.

HOT TIP: Note that only the names of the font-families are separated by commas in the font declaration!

Underline text

Underlining text used to be handled by the HTML `<u></u>` element, an inline formatting element. That element, however, is deprecated and not universally supported any longer. To facilitate underlining, CSS provides the text-decoration: underline property declaration. This places an underline beneath all text in the formatted element(s).

1 Create a blank style.css file in your text editor.

2 Add a declaration to set the `<body>` element with the underline property:
`text-decoration: underline;`

3 Save and close the CSS file.

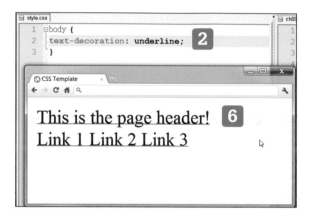

4 Open the HTML template in your text editor and add a `<link />` tag to the `<head>` element.

5 Set the href value to the style.css file you just created.

6 Save the HTML file with a new name and open it in your web browser.

? DID YOU KNOW?

Note that CSS applies formatting to *all* the text in an element. This may not always be desirable, especially when underlining text, which is generally done in small sections or for a few sentences. It may be more practical to use an inline style declared in the start tag of an inline element, such as the `<ins>` tag, rather than declaring a CSS rule.

? DID YOU KNOW?

It may be necessary to remove other formatting elements to make formatting changes visible, depending on how the browser handles inheritance of element properties.

Overline text

Overlining, or overstriking, is mostly used in mathematics. It usually indicates a repeating decimal, a line segment, or a sample mean. It can also indicate logical OR and AND operators. The overline is created with the text-decoration: overline property declaration.

1 Create a new style.css file in your text editor.

2 Add a declaration to set the `<body>` element with the overline property: `text-decoration: overline;`

3 Save the CSS file and close it.

4 Open the HTML template in your text editor and add the `<link />` tag to the `<head>` element.

5 Set the href value to the style.css file you just created.

6 Save the HTML document with a new name and open it in your web browser.

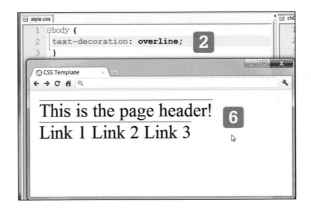

? DID YOU KNOW?

There is little need for the use of overline outside of specialised content. But creative use of one formatting construct for additional purposes is part of web design!

? DID YOU KNOW?

Much useful information on how to properly use overline formatting is available on the Internet. Use your favourite search engine to search for 'overline text' and see for yourself!

Line-through text content

In legal matters, or matters where original wording retention is critical, rather than replacing content, strikethrough is used to indicate deleted content. In CSS, the text-decoration declaration provides the line-through property for this purpose. It can also be used to show tongue-in-cheek re-wording for web pages with a more casual and humorous bent.

1 Using your text editor, create a new, blank style.css file.

2 Add a declaration to set the `<body>` element to line-through: `text-decoration: line-through;`

3 Save and close the style.css file.

4 Open the HTML template in your text editor and add a `<link />` tag to the `<head>` element.

5 Set the href value to the style.css file you just saved.

6 Save the HTML document with a new name and open it in your web browser.

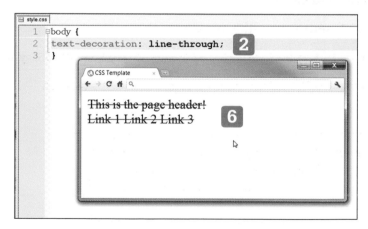

? DID YOU KNOW?
Line-through will apply to all text content in a given element when applied. Handle its use with care.

🔥 HOT TIP: If you only want to line-through a few words, or a sentence, it may be easier to simply use the `<del></del>` HTML element instead of declaring a CSS property for an entire element.

Make text blink

Text decoration is a tricky proposal. The object is to make the text stand out and be striking, but not annoying. The ability to make text blink on the page has a long and chequered history in HTML, but the capability carries on with CSS. The text-decoration declaration provides the blink property to flash text on- and off-screen.

1 Create a new style.css file in your text editor.

2 Add a declaration for the `<body>` element and set the blink property: `text-decoration: blink;`

```
style.css
1 body {
2 text-decoration: blink; 2
3 }
```

3 Save the CSS file and close it.

4 Open your HTML template with your text editor.

5 Add the `<link />` tag and set the href value to the style.css file you just created.

6 Save and close the HTML file and open it in your web browser.

 HOT TIP: Blinking text may seem a novel idea initially, but it can be extremely annoying for a visitor to have the words on a page flashing in their face. The blink pace and position of the flashing text are critical. Use this CSS tool with caution!

? **DID YOU KNOW?**
At the time of writing, the blink property decoration did not function in Google Chrome (version 12.0.742.100), but did work in an older version of Mozilla Firefox (version 3.6.17). It may not function in all browsers, so test before deploying!

Make text uppercase

Many headings and footers are set apart from the text content around them by how the text is formatted. Using all uppercase text, for instance, might be a good way to distinguish and call attention to a page header. CSS3 provides the text-transform declaration to change cases for text, and specifically the uppercase property value to change text to all uppercase letters for any element to which it's applied.

1 In your text editor, create a blank style.css file.

2 Add a `text-transform: uppercase;` declaration to the `<header>` element.

3 Save the CSS file and close it.

4 Open the HTML template with your text editor and add the `<link />` tag.

5 Set the href attribute to the style.css file you just made.

6 Save the HTML document and open it with your web browser.

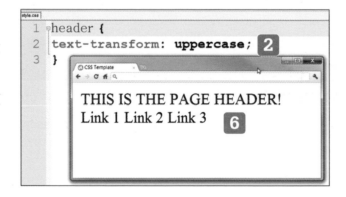

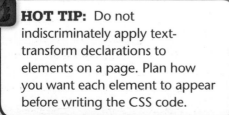

HOT TIP: Do not indiscriminately apply text-transform declarations to elements on a page. Plan how you want each element to appear before writing the CSS code.

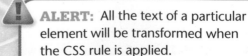

ALERT: All the text of a particular element will be transformed when the CSS rule is applied.

Make text lowercase

Text can be made all lowercase using the CSS text-transform declaration with the lowercase property value set. As with other text-transform properties, declare with caution since all text in a formatted element will be changed to lowercase when the property is applied.

1 Create a blank style.css file in your text editor.

2 Add a text-transform declaration and set the header text to lowercase:

```
text-transform: lowercase;
```

3 Save and close the CSS file.

4 Open the HTML template in your text editor.

5 Add the `<link />` tag to the `<head>` element and set the href attribute to the CSS file you just made.

6 Save the HTML document and open it in your web browser.

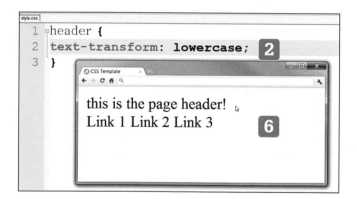

HOT TIP: Use the lowercase declaration on stylised pages to add a unique look to headings and navigational aids. It may not be appropriate for use in textual elements such as paragraphs, articles and sections.

HOT TIP: Use of lowercase heading elements on a page can offer a clean, minimalistic and professional appearance as well as a casual, more modern touch.

Capitalise each word of text content

To transform text to capitalise the first letter of each word, CSS provides the capitalise property value of the text-transform declaration. Each word in the formatted element receives a capitalised first letter, while the rest of the text remains unchanged.

1 Create a blank style.css file in your text editor.

2 Add a text-transform declaration and set the header text to capitalise:

```
text-transform: capitalize;
```

3 Save and close the CSS file.

4 Open the HTML template in your text editor.

5 Add the `<link />` tag to the `<head>` element and set the href attribute to the CSS file you just made.

6 Save the HTML document and open it in your web browser.

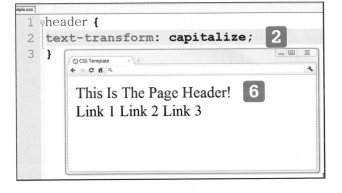

```
style.css
1  header {
2    text-transform: capitalize;  2
3  }
```

CSS Template

This Is The Page Header! **6**
Link 1 Link 2 Link 3

 ALERT: Remember, use US spellings in all code or it won't work!

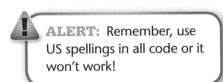 **HOT TIP:** A critical caveat to the use of the capitalise declaration is how all words are indiscriminately capitalised, which is not a true title case. When using capitalise, remember that all words will be capitalised, not just certain, key words as in title case capitalisation.

? DID YOU KNOW?

As with other text-transform property declarations, capitalise is probably best used in headings for sections, articles and the like. Capitalising the first letter for all words in an article or a blog entry would be distracting, unattractive and unprofessional. As usual, handle with care.

Add drop shadows to text

The text shadow creates a three-dimensional effect by adding a drop shadow behind text content. Varying the colour, diffusion (or spread) and distance from text creates wonderful effects, even text which appears aflame. The drop shadow is created with the text-shadow property, and values are for colour, distance from text and spread. For example:

```
text-shadow: 12px 10px 2px darkgray;
```

1 Create a blank style.css file in your text editor.

2 Create a drop-shadow declaration for the `<header>` element.

3 Make the shadow blue with a 5 pixel drop, a right offset of 5 pixels, and a 5 pixel spread: `text-shadow:5px 5px 5px blue;`

4 Save the style sheet and close it.

5 Open the HTML template in your text browser and add a `<link />` tag with the href set to the new CSS file.

6 Save the HTML file with a new name and open it in your web browser.

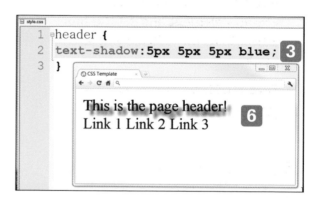

```
1  header {
2  text-shadow:5px 5px 5px blue; 3
3  }
```

This is the page header!
Link 1 Link 2 Link 3   6

? DID YOU KNOW?

Effects achievable with text shadow had to be done previously in graphics-editing or rendering software such as Adobe Photoshop®. But now CSS3 makes it accessible to anyone with a little creativity, a text editor and a browser. Experiment with offset distances and colours to find interesting and exciting combinations.

🔥 HOT TIP: Remember to use the hash symbol (#) before any hexadecimal colour code in the declaration, but leave it off if you use the colour name instead.

11 Controlling white space

Introduction

White space refers, literally, to the 'white', or blank or open, areas of a page. This term applies in both print media and on the screen.

White space provides the reader's eye with much needed space and rest areas, and can be used to focus attention and provide impact or emphasise specific content. If the page is too crowded and busy with images, text, video and decorations, it's not aesthetically pleasing. Increasing white space is one way to ease the crowding on a page and give a more pleasing visual experience.

White space includes how paragraphs are aligned, how content fits within the margins of an element, distance between lines of text and even between words and letters. By controlling white space you can make the difference between a busy page which doesn't retain readers, and a sharp, crisp, easy-to-read page which attracts and retains visitors.

Set element padding

An element's internal padding, or the space between the element's content and its border, is set with the CSS padding property. The declaration p {padding: 5px;} assigns a 5 pixel padding between the paragraph's text and border on all sides. Each side can also be set individually using the same declaration, or with use of individual declarations.

1 Create a new style.css file in your text editor.

2 Add a declaration to set the `<header>` element padding to 20px: `padding: 20px;`

3 Save the style sheet and close it.

4 Open your HTML template in your text editor.

5 Add a `<link />` tag to the `<head>` element with the href value set to the style.css file you just created.

6 Save the HTML file with a new name and open it in your web browser.

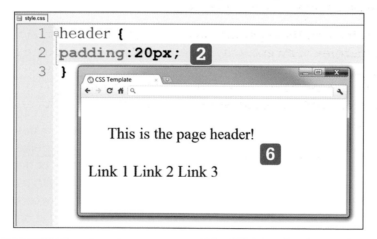

```
style.css

1  header {
2  padding:20px;  2
3  }
```

CSS Template

This is the page header!
6

Link 1 Link 2 Link 3

 HOT TIP: As with other selectors, combinators could be used to format *only* the precise elements targeted. If you're interested in finding out about those combinators and selectors, consult the Quick Reference Guide from www.veign.com or any online CSS3 resource for more information.

 DID YOU KNOW?

When using the padding single declaration, the order of sides is top, right, bottom, left (padding: topvalue rightvalue bottomvalue leftvalue). So a single declaration with 2px of padding at the top and bottom and 20px at the left and right would read: padding: 2px 20px 2px 20px; Again, the more efficient the code, the better and more legible it will be.

Set element margins

Elements have a right, left, top and bottom margin. Margins, like padding and many other CSS properties, can be set either separately or together in one declaration. A margin's width may be a length (in pixels), a percentage or auto. As with other elements, length is a fixed measurement and percentage refers to the margin's parent element. Auto allows the browser to determine the margin.

1 Create a new style.css file in your text editor.

2 Add a declaration setting the `<header>` top margin to 50 pixels: `margin: 50px 0px 0px 0px;`

3 Save the style.css file and close it.

4 Open the HTML template with your text editor.

5 Add a `<link />` tag to the `<head>` element with the href value set to the newly created style.css file.

6 Save the HTML document with a new name and open it in your web browser.

> **? DID YOU KNOW?**
> If two elements had a 5 pixel margin, the total space between them would be 10 pixels.

> **? DID YOU KNOW?**
> Margins can be eliminated to butt adjacent elements together or increased to add white space to the overall page. The desired effect will determine whether to increase or decrease margins just as with padding. It may also be necessary to increase padding in one area and reduce it on another side to create the desired look.

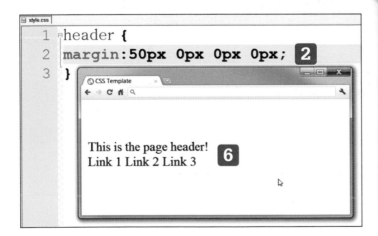

```
style.css
1  header {
2  margin:50px 0px 0px 0px;   2
3  }
```

This is the page header!
Link 1 Link 2 Link 3   **6**

WHAT DOES THIS MEAN?

Margin: the space between elements. It's a cushion around an element's border which no other elements may pass.

Align text to the left

CSS3 provides the ability to align along the left margin with the text-align: left property declaration. Left-aligned is the default for all web browsers with Western-based language bases, but CSS3 allows the alignment to be specified if need be.

1 Use your text editor to create a new, blank style.css file.

2 Add a text-align declaration for the `<header>` element and set its value to 'left':
`text-align: left;`

3 Save and close the style.css file.

4 Use your text editor to open the HTML template.

5 Add the `<link />` tag and set the href value to the style.css file you just created.

6 Save the HTML document with a new name and open it in your web browser.

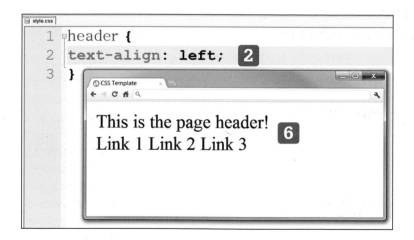

```
style.css
1  header {
2  text-align: left;   2
3  }
```

CSS Template

This is the page header!   6
Link 1 Link 2 Link 3

 DID YOU KNOW?
Left justification is the default for all HTML elements with Western-based languages.

HOT TIP: Using text alignment to create interest can have quite an impact. As in all things, however, over-indulgence can be problematic. Use text alignment judiciously.

Align text to the right

Text can be aligned along the right margin of a page rather than the left margin to create interest. CSS3 provides the 'right' value for the text-align property declaration for this purpose. In this mode, the text is lined up along the right-hand edge of the content, and the left edge is ragged.

1 Use your text editor to create a new, blank style.css file.

2 Add a text-align declaration for the `<header>` element and set its value to 'right':
`text-align: right;`

3 Save and close the style.css file.

4 Use your text editor to open the HTML template.

5 Add the `<link />` tag and set the href value to the style.css file you just created.

6 Save the HTML document with a new name and open it in your web browser.

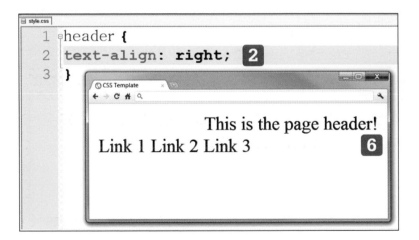

 HOT TIP: Right-aligned text can completely change the look and feel of a site with one simple declaration.

? **DID YOU KNOW?**

The default alignment for Western-based languages is left-to-right, but for languages naturally oriented right-to-left, the browser and operating system regional settings will come into play. Investigate how the page looks if you're working with a right-to-left language before you declare a CSS property to align the text.

Centre-align text

Text can be centred between the margins, which is referred to as centre alignment, using the text-align declaration's center property. All the characters in a line of text content are centred on the page rather than aligned along the left or right margins. Headings are often centre-aligned on a page over their content.

1 Use your text editor to create a new, blank style.css file.

2 Add a text-align declaration for the `<header>` element and set its value to 'center':
`text-align: center;`

3 Save and close the style.css file.

4 Use your text editor to open the HTML template.

5 Add the `<link />` tag and set the href value to the style.css file you just created.

6 Save the HTML document with a new name and open it in your web browser.

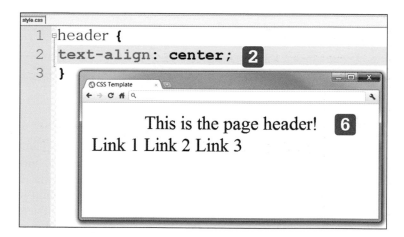

ALERT: Note the US spelling of 'center', rather than 'centre'. The property declaration will not work with a UK spelling. Remember, spelling counts in code!

HOT TIP: As with any text-decoration property, use centre alignment carefully so as not to overwhelm the user or overdo the technique. A website with too many text-decoration 'tricks' seems amateurish and the effects can be a distraction rather than an aid to viewing.

Justify text between margins

Spacing text evenly so both the left and right margins are aligned is called justified text. CSS3 permits text justification using the text-align declaration's justify property value setting. Each line is stretched to have equal width across the space allotted for the content. This is common in newspaper and magazine print.

1 Use your text editor to create a new, blank style.css file.

2 Add a text-align declaration for the `<header>` element and set its value to 'justify':
`text-align: justify;`

3 Save and close the style.css file.

4 Use your text editor to open the HTML template.

5 Add the `<link />` tag and set the href value to the style.css file you just created.

6 Save the HTML document with a new name and open it in your web browser.

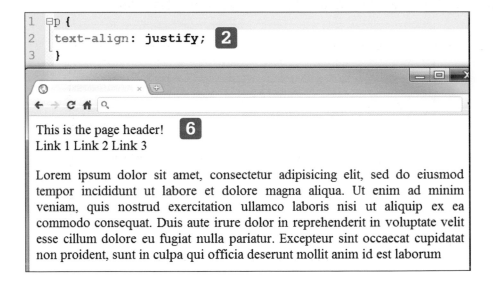

```
1  p {
2    text-align: justify;   2
3  }
```

This is the page header!   **6**
Link 1 Link 2 Link 3

Lorem ipsum dolor sit amet, consectetur adipisicing elit, sed do eiusmod tempor incididunt ut labore et dolore magna aliqua. Ut enim ad minim veniam, quis nostrud exercitation ullamco laboris nisi ut aliquip ex ea commodo consequat. Duis aute irure dolor in reprehenderit in voluptate velit esse cillum dolore eu fugiat nulla pariatur. Excepteur sint occaecat cupidatat non proident, sunt in culpa qui officia deserunt mollit anim id est laborum

? DID YOU KNOW?

Most of the text-adjustment declarations used in this chapter are best reserved for headings.

? DID YOU KNOW?

The space between a declaration's property and the value setting is optional. Having it in or leaving it out has no impact on how the browser renders the text being formatted.

Adjust word spacing

Use of white space eases reading in print and on screen. To control white space effectively, CSS provides several adjustments including the space between words. Add white space between words with the word-spacing declaration. The valid settings for the property are normal, the length in point size, and percentages of the font.

1 Create a new style.css file in your text editor.

2 Add a word-spacing declaration for the `<header>` element with a value of 24pt:
`word-spacing: 24pt;`

3 Save the CSS file and close it.

4 Open your HTML template in your text editor.

5 Add a `<link />` tag to the `<head>` element and set the href value to the CSS file you just created.

6 Save the HTML document and open it in your web browser.

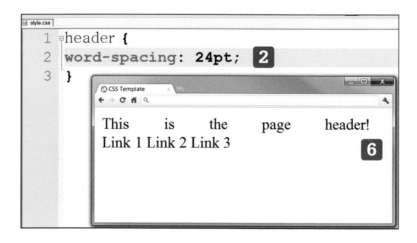

? **DID YOU KNOW?**
Getting carried away with white space will make the page as difficult to read as not having enough. Be judicious in your use of the word-spacing declaration to avoid pages with too much white space.

▶ **SEE ALSO:** See the Quick Reference Guide for CSS3 you downloaded from www.veign. com for a complete list of the text controls available in CSS, including white space controls.

Adjust letter spacing

CSS3 permits setting the white space between individual letters in a word. The letter-spacing declaration allows control over how much space is allowed between individual letters in a word. The valid settings are normal, a specified font point-size, or in pixels.

1 Create a new style.css file in your text editor.

2 Add a word-spacing declaration for the `<header>` element with a value of 25px:
`letter-spacing: 25px;`

3 Save the CSS file and close it.

4 Open your HTML template in your text editor.

5 Add a `<link />` tag to the `<head>` element and set the href value to the CSS file you just created.

6 Save the HTML document and open it in your web browser.

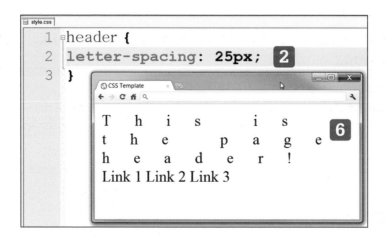

? DID YOU KNOW?

The use of white space between letters is trickier than using white space between words on a page. The eye is used to seeing and accepting some gap between the words. But when the space between the letters is increased or decreased too much it can be a distraction.

? DID YOU KNOW?

Experiment to find how much white space between letters in a word is acceptable to your eye. If you find it attractive it's very likely someone else will too.

Set line-wrapping

A paragraph's wrapping behaviour refers to how white space in the element is controlled and how lines of text content wrap to a new line. It can be set using the CSS white-space property. Valid values are normal, pre and nowrap. For example:

```
p {white-space:nowrap;}
```

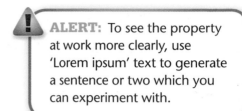

ALERT: To see the property at work more clearly, use 'Lorem ipsum' text to generate a sentence or two which you can experiment with.

Specifying pre preserves all white space. Specifying nowrap prevents text wrapping. A long line forces readers to scroll horizontally to read it.

1 Create a new style.css file in your text editor.

2 Add a `<header>` white-space declaration with a value of nowrap: `white-space: nowrap;`

3 Save and close the file.

4 Open your HTML template in your text editor and add a `<link />` tag to the `<head>` element.

5 Set the href attribute to the newly saved style. css file.

6 Save the HTML document with a new name and open it in your web browser.

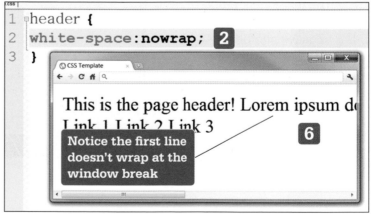

```
1  header {
2  white-space:nowrap;  2
3  }
```

This is the page header! Lorem ipsum d

Link 1 Link 2 Link 3   **6**

Notice the first line doesn't wrap at the window break

? DID YOU KNOW?

The white-space declaration has other settings which might be difficult to distinguish from one another. A good online tutorial is www.w3schools.com, which provides an excellent working 'lab' where you can see the various effects. Search for the white-space property on the site for more.

Set the text-indent property

Indenting text on the page offers the appearance of printed material such as a magazine or newspaper, or even a book. Indenting text is another way to offer white space and delineate between paragraphs. It's easy to read and with the text-indent property of CSS, easy to implement as well.

1 Use your text editor to create a blank style.css file and add a declaration to a `<p>` element to indent the text 20 pixels: `text-indent: 20px;`

2 Save the style sheet and close it.

3 Open your HTML editor in your text editor and add a `<link />` tag with the href value set to your new style sheet.

4 Add a paragraph of 'Lorem ipsum' text to the `<body>` element.

5 Save the HTML document with a new name and close it.

6 Open the HTML file in your web browser.

 DID YOU KNOW?

The text-indent property value is able to accept negative numbers, which will move the line to the left rather than to the right, sometimes referred to as 'outdenting' the text. This is one method for creating a 'hanging indent' for text in special circumstances.

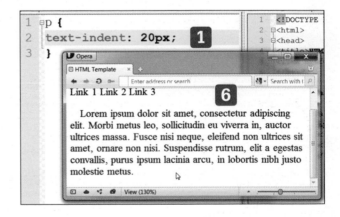

 DID YOU KNOW?

As with any property, use text-indent judiciously. Overuse of the property can be detrimental rather than beneficial to a page's appearance.

HOT TIP: The text-indent property works best with long blocks of inline content like paragraphs and block quotes.

12 Sizing elements with CSS

Introduction

Margins and padding work the same for HTML elements as they do for HTML tables cells, and you can think of elements on a web page as a type of cell. In this discussion, 'border' refers to the edge or boundary of an element, while 'padding' refers to the space between the content of an element and its border. 'Margin' refers to the space between element borders on a page.

Envisioning the elements on a web page as boxes composed of borders, margins and padding is referred to as the 'box model' in CSS. Using relative (in relation to the parent, or container element) or absolute (declaring definitively) measures you can size the elements on your page to highlight content the best way.

Set relative width

An element's width is declared with the width property. Values of auto, a length in pixels, or a percentage relative to the parent element are the settings.

When setting a relative width, the size of the element is determined in relationship to its parent. With a width of 50%, the width is 50% of the parent element.

1. Create a new style.css file with your text editor.

2. Add a declaration to set the width of the `<header>` element to 10%:
   width: 10%;

3. Save and close the style sheet file.

4. Open the HTML template in your text editor.

5. Add a `<link />` tag in the `<head>` element with the href value set to the new style.css file.

6. Save the HTML document with a new name and open it in your web browser.

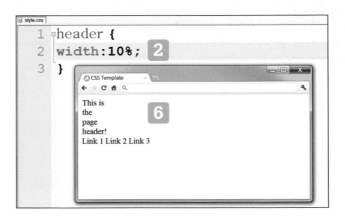

? DID YOU KNOW?

If the concept of relative sizing is confusing, think about it this way: the size setting for any element is relative to the container holding it. If the element is set to take up half the container, its size will depend on the size of the container holding it. A 50% width setting can be very large or very small depending on how large or small the container is. The element expands or contracts compared to the space allotted.

Set absolute width

When using a fixed measurement, an element's width and height are sized to the specified dimensions. The same declaration (width: *value*) is used, but instead of a percentage, a figure in pixels is used as the value to make the setting absolute, meaning it does not change as the parent resizes.

1 Create a new style.css file with your text editor.

2 Add a declaration to set the width of the `<header>` element to 50 pixels:
   `width: 50px;`

3 Save and close the style sheet file.

4 Open the HTML template in your text editor.

5 Add a `<link />` tag in the `<head>` element with the href value set to the new style.css file.

6 Save the HTML document with a new name and open it in your web browser.

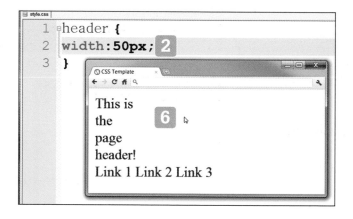

SEE ALSO: There are many other position and sizing elements available to web designers which make it possible to establish elements on a page with extreme precision. Check out CSS3 design sites and tutorials for more information.

? DID YOU KNOW?

Absolute length values define height and width regardless of the parent element's settings. Moreover, as the browser window is resized, elements with relative width and height settings resize themselves in relation to the browser. Elements with a fixed height and width do not.

Set an element's minimum width

Establishing a minimum width for an element means it will shrink only so far within the parent element (or the browser window). After that, the window will cut off the content. Setting minimum widths for elements is done with the min-width declaration. The values can be set either in percent (relative to the parent element) or in pixels (absolute setting), for example:

```
min-width: 50%;
```

1 Create a new style.css file with your text editor.

2 Add a declaration to set the minimum width of the `<header>` element to 100 pixels: `min-width:100px;`

3 Save and close the style sheet file.

4 Open the HTML template in your text editor.

5 Add a `<link />` tag in the `<head>` element with the href value set to the new style.css file.

6 Save the HTML file with a new name and open it in your web browser.

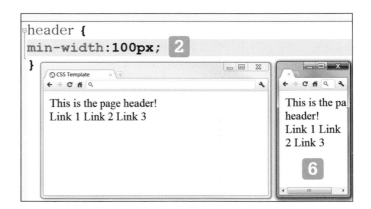

ALERT: To see this declaration in action, you need to shrink the browser window so the `<header>` element contracts below the minimum value.

HOT TIP: Be careful with the min-width declaration; it is possible to limit an element's width to make it impossible for a reader to see content without scrolling.

Set an element's maximum width

Setting the maximum width of an element limits how far it will expand on the screen. It can be set to a relative measure (which is a percentage of the parent element) or a fixed measure (or absolute value). The element will never grow beyond the limit set. The maximum width is declared with max-width.

1 Create a new style.css file with your text editor.

2 Add a declaration to set the maximum width of the `<header>` element to 50 pixels: `max-width:50px;`

3 Save and close the style sheet file.

4 Open the HTML template in your text editor.

5 Add a `<link />` tag in the `<head>` element with the href value set to the new style.css file.

6 Save the HTML document with a new name and open it in your web browser.

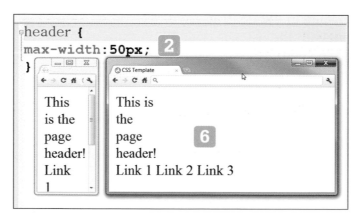

 ALERT: To view the results of the max-width declaration, expand your browser window beyond the setting to notice how the element will not grow beyond the value set.

 HOT TIP: Be careful when setting width for an element. Remember, many modern computer screens are much wider than they are tall. It's easy to make the width incompatible or silly by setting the width of a page or element incorrectly. Be sure to test any coding with several screen sizes if possible.

Set relative height

Setting relative height makes sure an element's height is set in comparison to the element around it (or the containing element, or parent element). The height for an element is declared with the height property and the value used is in a percentage of the parent element, for example:

```
height: 20%;
```

1 Create a new style.css file with your text editor.

2 Add an image declaration and set the height to 10% of the parent element: `img {height:10%;}`

3 Save and close the CSS file.

4 Open your HTML template in the text editor and add an image to the body element.

5 Save the HTML document with a new name.

6 Open the HTML file in your web browser.

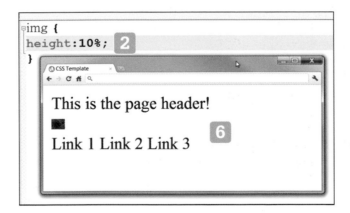

SEE ALSO: See the 'Add images to a web page' section in Chapter 4 for information on how to insert an image in an HTML document.

HOT TIP: Be very careful with the height of an element. Most modern computer screens are much wider than tall, and if the height is not set correctly the page could appear very strange to a visitor. It's good general practice to test any coding with several screens or resolutions if possible.

Set absolute height

Absolute height is set using the same property declaration as with relative height. The only difference is the units specified; instead of a percentage of the parent element's height, the measure is a fixed height in pixels. The absolute height setting prevents an element from expanding beyond its set limits.

1. Create a new style.css file with your text editor.

2. Add a declaration to set the height of the `<header>` element to 10 pixels: `height: 10px;`

3. Save and close the style sheet file.

4. Open the HTML template in your text editor.

5. Add a `<link />` tag in the `<head>` element with the href value set to the new style.css file.

6. Save the HTML document with a new name and open it in your web browser.

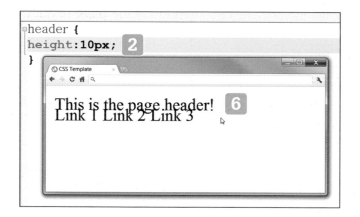

 HOT TIP: Note the text size within the affected element didn't change; only the size of the rendering box for the element changes. In this case, the `<nav>` element text begins to overlap the `<header>` element text.

? **DID YOU KNOW?**

Most of the effects from the height property declaration are seen on images, but they affect all elements.

Set an element's minimum height

Establishing a minimum height for an element means it will shrink only so far within the parent element (or the browser window). After that, the window will cut off the content. Setting minimum heights for elements is done with the min-height declaration. The values can be set in either percent (relative to the parent element) or in pixels (absolute setting), for example:

```
min-height: 50%;
```

1 Create a new style.css file with your text editor.

2 Add a declaration to set the minimum height of the `<header>` element to 50 pixels: `min-height:50px;`

3 Save and close the style sheet file.

4 Open the HTML template in your text editor.

5 Add a `<link />` tag in the `<head>` element with the href value set to the new style.css file.

6 Save the HTML file with a new name and open it in your web browser.

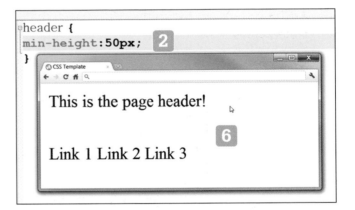

 ALERT: As a precaution, test any min-height settings with multiple monitors and resolutions if possible to ensure there are no unexpected results on screen.

 DID YOU KNOW?
Setting a minimum size for an element can help preserve content integrity. If it's important for the content to be displayed at a certain size, including aspect ratio, it might be wise to use minimum size settings to ensure the content displays properly.

HOT TIP: Remember, many computer monitors are wider than taller now, and height can become a tricky property to set!

Set an element's maximum height

Setting the maximum height of an element limits how far it will lengthen. It can be a relative measure (which is a percentage of the parent element) or a fixed measure (or absolute value). The element will never extend past the established limit. The maximum height is declared with max-height.

1 Create a new style.css file with your text editor.

2 Add a declaration to set the maximum height of the <header> element to 10 pixels: max-height:10px;

3 Save and close the style sheet file.

4 Open the HTML template in your text editor.

5 Add a <link /> tag in the <head> element with the href value set to the new style.css file.

6 Save the HTML document with a new name and open it in your web browser.

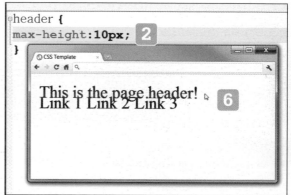

 ALERT: To view the results of the max-height declaration, make your browser window longer than the setting to see the element stays at the value set.

 HOT TIP: With a wide-aspect screen, it may be necessary to set the maximum element height to a shorter length than for screens which have the older 4:3 aspect ratio.

WHAT DOES THIS MEAN?

Aspect ratio: a computer or TV screen's width-to-height ratio, in pixels.

13 Positioning elements with CSS

Introduction

Envisioning the elements on a web page as boxes composed of borders, margins and padding is referred to as the 'box model' in CSS. Specific elements can be positioned on a page with precision to create logical, natural content flow. Unless specifically instructed otherwise, a browser will position elements as they appear on the HTML file for the page. That is, they're positioned as the browser encounters them. In short, a browser reads and displays elements left-to-right, top-to-bottom, unless instructed otherwise by CSS code. CSS provides instructions to position elements in absolute, relative or fixed positions, and for positioning elements beside other elements.

Position elements with float

The float property moves an element as far to the right or left as possible within the element's parent. Specifying float right (float:right) instructs browsers to place other elements on the floated element's left. Specifying float left (float:left) places elements on the floated element's right.

1 Create a new style.css file in your text editor.

2 Add a rule for the `<aside>` element with the float set to 'right'.

3 Save the style sheet and close it.

4 Open the HTML template and add a `<link />` tag with the href set to the newly created style sheet.

5 Add content to the `<aside>` and `<section>` elements identifying the two elements.

6 Save the HTML file and open it in your web browser.

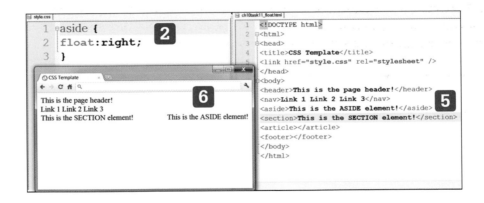

HOT TIP: The content in the elements added in step 5 is for visual clarity. This will help you see how the float property works.

 DID YOU KNOW?

You could add declarations to your style sheet to modify the text in each element to make it distinguishable by colour, font-size, background colour or image, etc. Even adding a border to the elements might make them more easily visible on screen. Do whatever it takes to practise your coding skills!

Position elements with clear

The clear property specifies an element may not have another element float to its left, right or both. With clear, the element is displayed on its own line with nothing to the cleared side. If 'both' is set as the value, the element appears as if it were a block element.

1 Create a new style.css file with your text editor.

2 Add a rule for the `<p>` element with the clear property set to value 'both':
`p {clear:both;}`

3 Add a rule for the `<img>` tag and set the float to 'left': `img {float:left;}`

4 Save the CSS file and close it.

5 Open the HTML template in your text editor.

6 Add a `<link />` tag to the `<head>` element with the href set to the newly saved style.css file.

7 Add an image to the `<body>` element and a `<p>` element with content (I used the phrase 'This is text' repeated).

8 Save the HTML document with a new name and open it in your web browser.

? DID YOU KNOW?

If you set the float property as in step 3 but do not use the clear property for the `<p>` element, the text will be positioned beside the image on the page.

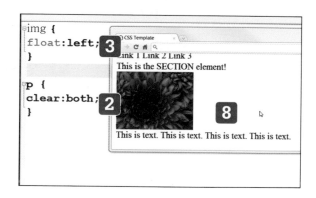

? DID YOU KNOW?

The clear property and the float property are meant to work hand-in-hand with one another. To make them really shine, add an image to the HTML document and set float to 'left' in the style sheet file. Save both documents and load the HTML file into your web browser for a clearer view of the effects they can have.

Set absolute positioning for elements

In order to use the placement of an element, you must first tell the browser whether you are placing it relative to the original position in the HTML document, or whether you are specifying it absolutely. The position property is used for this purpose. Set the value to absolute to dictate absolutely where on the page the element should fall.

1 Open your text editor and create a blank style.css file.

2 Add a declaration to set the `<header>` element's position setting to absolute: `position:absolute;`

3 Save the style sheet and close it.

4 Open the HTML template in your text editor.

5 Add the `<link />` element to the style sheet you just made.

6 Save the HTML file with a new name and launch it in your web browser.

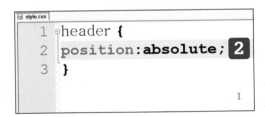

? **DID YOU KNOW?**

The absolute position is still relative – relative to the first parent element with a position set. If there is no positioned parent, then it's relative to the `<html>` element of the page.

? **DID YOU KNOW?**

The positioning declarations for specific sides of an element, such as top and left, are covered next in their own sections in this chapter.

Position the top of an element

The top property declares how far from the top of the page or the parent element the browser places the top edge of an element. Positive values move the element down the page; negative values move the image up the page. The element's position is based on the parent element's position. A setting of 20px from the top will be 20px from the top regardless of how large the page is.

1 Create a new style.css file with your text editor.

2 Add a declaration to position the `<header>` element 80px from the top with absolute positioning: `position:absolute; top:80px;`

3 Save the style sheet and close it.

4 Open your HTML template in your text editor.

5 Add a `<link />` element to the style sheet you just created.

6 Save and close the HTML file, then open it with your web browser.

DID YOU KNOW?

You could also set the value of the position in percentage of the parent element.

The concept of the absolute position is actually less intuitive than the relative positioning. Just remember the absolute position doesn't change, even if the browser window is resized. The absolute position is a setting on the browser window or in the parent element, with no regard for where the HTML document places the element. With relative positioning, the position is relative to the *original* element position, i.e. where it falls in the HTML document.

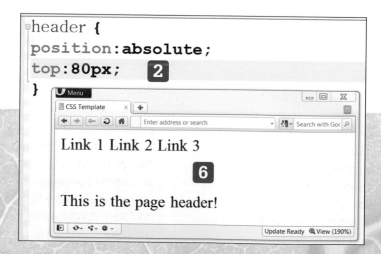

Position an element's right side

The right property determines how far from the right of the page the right edge of the element is placed. Positive values cause the element to shift right; negative values shift it left. The values can be either pixels or a percentage of the container element. This setting is used alongside the position property setting to determine how to position the element's right side relative to the parent element's position.

1 Create a new style.css file with your text editor.

2 Add a declaration to absolute position the `<header>` element 50px from the right: position: `absolute; right:50px;`

3 Save the style sheet and close it.

4 Open your HTML template in your text editor.

5 Add a `<link />` element to the style sheet you just created.

6 Save and close the HTML file, then open it with your web browser.

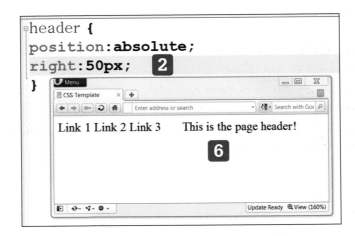

HOT TIP: Play with the zoom and window size in your browser and watch how the `<header>` element moves on the page according to the value you set in the declaration.

HOT TIP: Open the HTML template and save it with a `<link />` element in the `<head>` element, and set the href attribute to the location where you saved the style.css file. Then all you have to do is open the HTML document and save it with a new name. All the other steps are taken care of!

Position an element's left side

The left property determines how far from the left page edge the left element's edge is positioned. Positive numbers cause the element to shift left; negative values shift it right. The values can be either pixels or a percentage of the container element. It's used alongside the position property setting to determine how to position the element's left side relative to the parent element's position.

1 Create a new style.css file with your text editor.

2 Add a declaration to absolute position the `<header>` element 50px from the left:
`position:absolute; left:50px;`

3 Save the style sheet and close it.

4 Open your HTML template in your text editor.

5 Add a `<link />` element to the style sheet you just created.

6 Save and close the HTML file, then open it with your web browser.

? DID YOU KNOW?

A browser reads and displays elements from an HTML document left-to-right, top-to-bottom, unless instructed otherwise by CSS code.

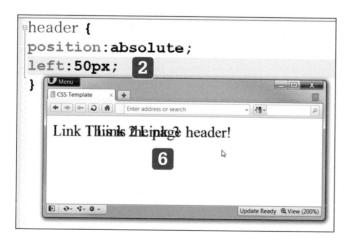

! ALERT: Be very careful in setting absolute values for positioning elements! The elements can overlap and produce very unexpected results or illegible content.

? DID YOU KNOW?

The units for the values are set in CSS units (px, em or cm), which are pixels (px), font-size relative (em, where 1em is the current font size) or centimetres (cm). The values can also be set in percentages (%) of the parent element's dimensions.

Position an element's bottom side

The top property declares how far from the bottom of the page or the parent element the browser places the lower edge of an element. Positive values move the element up the page; negative values move it down the page. It's used alongside the position property setting to determine how to position the element's bottom side relative to the parent element's position.

1 Create a new style.css file with your text editor.

2 Add a declaration to absolute position the `<header>` element 50px from the bottom: `position:absolute; bottom:50px;`

3 Save the style sheet and close it.

4 Open your HTML template in your text editor.

5 Add a `<link />` element to the style sheet you just created.

6 Save and close the HTML file, then open it with your web browser.

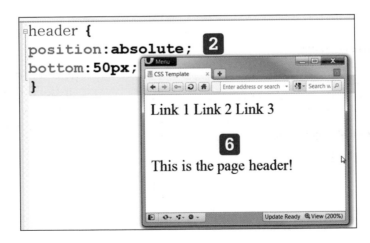

? **DID YOU KNOW?**
Block-level elements place content into a 'block' separate from other content, such as the `<h1>` to `<h6>` elements, and are placed top to bottom on their own line(s) as the browser reads them from the HTML file. Inline elements maintain content position while formatting it, such as the `<b>` or `<i>` tags, and are placed left to right on the lines in which they appear.

Set relative positioning

Similar to declaring an absolute position, declaring relative positioning is done with the position property. Set the value to relative to display the element's position relative to its normal (or *static*) position, which is where it will appear based on where in the HTML document it's placed.

1 Open your text editor and create a blank style.css file.

2 Add a declaration to set the `<header>` element's position setting to relative:
`position:relative;`

3 Save the style sheet and close it.

4 Open the HTML template in your text editor.

5 Add the `<link />` element to the style sheet you just made.

6 Save the HTML file with a new name and launch it in your web browser.

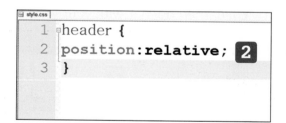

? DID YOU KNOW?

The absolute position is still relative – relative to the first parent element with a position set. If there is no positioned parent, then it's relative to the `<html>` element of the page.

? DID YOU KNOW?

Elements which may not be block elements ordinarily can be displayed as block elements using CSS. See the 'Position elements with float' and 'Position elements with clear' sections in this chapter for more information.

Use relative element positioning

Relative positioning allows an element to be positioned relative to its normal position, as determined by a browser. Relative positioning specifies how many pixels left, right, above or below an element's normal position it will be placed using the left, right, top and bottom offsets. Values for the settings can be a set measure such as pixels, or a percentage.

▶ **SEE ALSO:** See the 'Set relative positioning' section in this chapter for more details on declaring relative element positioning.

1 Create a new style.css file in your text editor.

2 Add a declaration to place the `<header>` element's left edge 30% left relative to its normal position: `position:relative; left:30%;`

3 Save the style sheet and close it.

4 Open the HTML template with your text editor and add a `<link />` tag to the style sheet you just made.

5 Save the HTML file with a new name and launch it in your web browser.

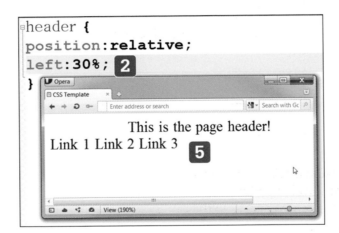

 DID YOU KNOW?
You could also specify more than one placement declaration to make the position more precise, such as top: 20px; right: -5px;.

 DID YOU KNOW?
You could have used a negative number for the value of a property to get a similar effect to using the opposing property. For example, using a negative top value has the same effect as a positive bottom value.

Fixed element positioning

Fixed position is similar to absolute positioning, except the element's position is fixed relative to the browser window. The parent container is irrelevant in this case. The element remains in its fixed position relative to the browser window regardless of size. Scrolling has no effect on the element either; it remains in one spot as the rest of the content scrolls. It is by using this property that pages can set a background image which doesn't scroll off-screen.

1 Open the style.css file with your text editor.

2 Add a declaration for the `<header>` element to fix the position: `position:fixed;`

3 Save the style sheet and open the HTML file in your web browser to view the results.

4 Open your HTML template in your text editor and add the `<link />` tag to your style.css file.

5 Add enough 'Lorem ipsum' text to the various elements to make sure a page will go past the browser window limits.

6 Save the HTML file with a new name and open it in your web browser.

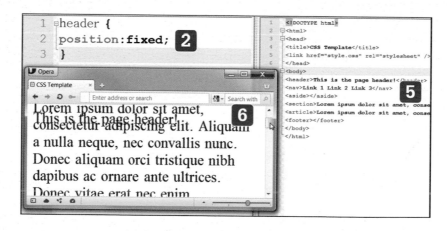

 HOT TIP: This is a great 'trick' to keep a piece of content in front of a user's view on a page!

? **DID YOU KNOW?**
If the content of your HTML file doesn't go beyond the browser's vertical limits, simply resize the window until the vertical scroll bar appears.

14 Formatting tables with CSS

Introduction

As powerful as tables are as tools, tabular data presentation is rather boring. To be able to make it less so, CSS provides table formatting properties.

Like most other elements in an HTML document, CSS formatting can be applied to many aspects of a table's structure. Borders can be manipulated, captions can be moved, layouts can be shifted and even the way that empty cells are displayed can be formatted.

When coupled with things such as font-sizes, weights, border colouring and all the other things CSS can do to affect the appearance of a web page, the final touches on a table can set off the tabular data so that it's not only less boring, but outright attractive.

Collapse table borders

HTML tables have both an inside and an outside border on all sides of a data cell. Collapsing borders means eliminating the separation between the two. When collapsed, the two borders become a single border around the element.

1 Use your text editor to create a new style.css file.

2 Set all table and cell element borders to 1px, solid-line, black, and set the borders to collapse: `border: 1px solid black; border-collapse: collapse;`

3 Save and close the CSS file.

4 Open the HTML template and add a `<link />` tag to the style sheet you just created.

5 Add a table to the page's body with three rows and three columns, with data in the cells.

6 Save the HTML document with a new name and open it in your web browser.

> ▶ **SEE ALSO:** See Chapter 5, 'Working with HTML tables', for more information on creating tables, table rows and table cells.

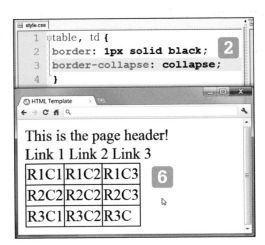

```
style.css
1  table, td {
2    border: 1px solid black;      2
3    border-collapse: collapse;
4  }
```

```
HTML Template
← → C ⌂ Q

This is the page header!
Link 1 Link 2 Link 3
┌────┬────┬────┐
│R1C1│R1C2│R1C3│   6
├────┼────┼────┤
│R2C2│R2C2│R2C3│
├────┼────┼────┤
│R3C1│R3C2│R3C │
└────┴────┴────┘
```

> **?** **DID YOU KNOW?**
> Using the border-collapse property is simple and effective, but there are other ways to achieve the same goal. Just as with most other things, there is more than one way to accomplish tasks. Using the border properties in CSS will also enable similar results. See Chapter 9, 'Setting borders and colours with CSS', for details.

Separate table borders

Table border separation is the default behaviour for the element, and it need not be specified under most circumstances. It may be necessary to do so from time to time, however, and it's accomplished with the border-collapse property value set to separate.

1 Use your text editor to create a new style.css file.

2 Set table and cell borders to 1px, solid-line black, and border-collapse to separate:
`border: 1px solid black; border-collapse: separate;`

3 Save and close the CSS file.

4 Open the HTML template and add a `<link />` tag to the style sheet you just created.

5 Create a table in the body element with three rows and three columns.

6 Save the HTML document with a new name and open it in your web browser.

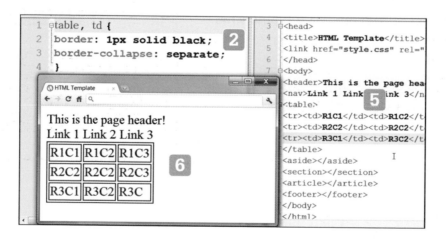

? DID YOU KNOW?

The border-collapse property doesn't provide any way to set the distance of the borders from one another. That is accomplished with the border-spacing properties, covered in later sections of this chapter.

▶ SEE ALSO: A similar effect can be achieved with other border properties in CSS, and even by setting table border attributes in the HTML tags. See Chapter 5, 'Working with HTML tables', and Chapter 9, 'Setting borders and colours with CSS', for more information and specifics.

Set the horizontal border spacing

Set the space between horizontal borders using the border-spacing property. The first value spacing sets the horizontal value, and the second sets the vertical value. If only one number is used, it sets both values.

1. Create a new style sheet in your text editor.

2. Add a declaration to set table and cell borders to 1px, solid, black: `border: 1px solid black;`

3. Add a declaration to set horizontal spacing to 30px: `border-spacing: 30px, 0px;`

4. Save and close the style sheet.

5. Open your HTML template, add a `<link />` tag to link to your new style sheet.

6. Add a table with three columns and rows in the `<body>` element and put content in each cell.

7. Save the HTML document with a new name and open it in your web browser.

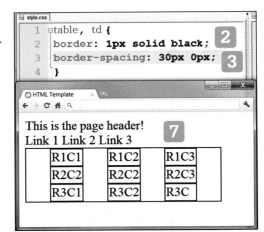

 DID YOU KNOW?
In this task it's not necessary to specify the border-collapse:separate property value since separate borders is the default value. We only need to specify that the table has borders.

HOT TIP: Since the tasks in this chapter all use a table as their basis, you can create a second HTML template by adding a table, and saving the document with the name Table_Template.html, and eliminate the step of creating one for each exercise. Alternatively you can recycle the files from the previous exercise whenever possible.

Set the vertical border spacing

Setting the vertical spacing is almost exactly like setting the horizontal spacing. The difference is in the property value you provide. The first number in the setting is the horizontal setting, the second the vertical setting.

1 Create a new style sheet in your text editor.

2 Add a declaration to set table and cell borders to 1px, solid, black and with vertical spacing to 30px: `border: 1px solid black; border-spacing: 0px 30px;`

3 Save and close the style sheet.

4 Open your HTML template, add a `<link />` tag to link to your new style sheet.

5 Add a table with three columns and rows in the `<body>` element.

6 Save the HTML document with a new name and open it in your web browser.

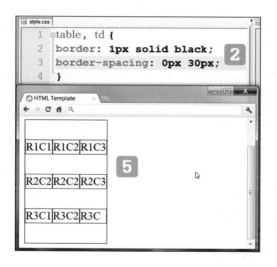

```
style.css
1  table, td {
2    border: 1px solid black;
3    border-spacing: 0px 30px;
4  }
```

 ALERT: If you're trying to *only* set the vertical value, be sure to set the horizontal value to 0, or the number you provide for the vertical value is applied to both settings!

? DID YOU KNOW?

Almost any value for the border-spacing attribute allowable is valid. Use measures like inches, centimetres or pixels, etc. Consult your Veign. com 'Quick Reference Guide for CSS3' for a list of measures permitted in CSS, and experiment.

Put a table caption below the table

Placement of the caption for a table isn't configurable with HTML markup alone. No matter where the `<caption>` element goes, the table caption is positioned in the same place. To adjust the caption position, CSS provides the caption-side property. Set the value to bottom and the caption will be placed below the table.

1 Create a new style.css file with your text editor.

2 Set table and cell borders to 1px, solid black and place the caption below the table:
`caption-side:bottom;`

3 Save and close the style sheet.

4 Open your HTML template and add a table with three rows and columns to the body of the document.

5 Add a `<caption>` element with 'Table caption text' as content inside the `<table>` element, before the cells.

6 Save the HTML document with a new name and open it in your web browser.

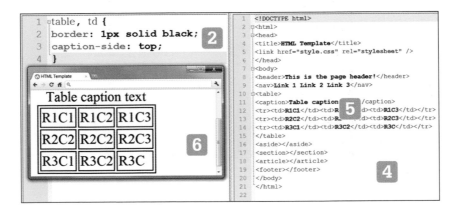

▶ **SEE ALSO:** See Chapter 5, 'Working with HTML tables', for further information on creating and captioning tables.

? **DID YOU KNOW?**
The default setting for the table caption placement is above the table.

Place a table caption above the table

Sometimes the caption for a table is best suited to precede the table, as a way of introducing the material in the table. Place the table caption above the table by using the caption-side property. Set the value to top and the caption will be placed above the table.

1 Create a new style.css file with your text editor.

2 Set table and cell borders to 1px, solid black and place the caption above the table: `caption-side: top;`

3 Save and close the style sheet.

4 Open your HTML template and add a table with three rows and columns to the body of the document.

5 Add a `<caption>` element with 'Table caption text' as content inside the `<table>` element, before the cells.

6 Save the HTML document with a new name and open it in your web browser.

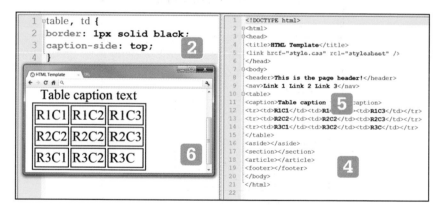

```
1  table, td {
2    border: 1px solid black;
3    caption-side: top;          2
4  }
```

```
1   <!DOCTYPE html>
2   <html>
3   <head>
4   <title>HTML Template</title>
5   <link href="style.css" rel="stylesheet" />
6   </head>
7   <body>
8   <header>This is the page header!</header>
9   <nav>Link 1 Link 2 Link 3</nav>
10  <table>
11  <caption>Table caption     5    caption>
12  <tr><td>R1C1</td><td>R1     <td>R1C3</td></tr>
13  <tr><td>R2C2</td><td>R2C2</td><td>R2C3</td></tr>
14  <tr><td>R3C1</td><td>R3C2</td><td>R3C</td></tr>
15  </table>
16  <aside></aside>
17  <section></section>
18  <article></article>          4
19  <footer></footer>
20  </body>
21  </html>
22
```

HTML Template

Table caption text

R1C1	R1C2	R1C3
R2C2	R2C2	R2C3
R3C1	R3C2	R3C

6

? DID YOU KNOW?

The top placement is the default behaviour for a table caption. In reality, there will be little cause to specify the top position. But in the case of interference with position from inherited behaviour from a parent element, it's always beneficial to know how to accomplish these things.

? DID YOU KNOW?

The `<caption>` element for a table is placed inside the table itself, before any of the table rows and columns. Because the caption is nested within the table it captions, there is no ambiguity about which caption goes with which table in markup code.

Hide empty table cells

It is possible to hide cells in a table structure which do not contain any data. This helps the eye flow over the tabular layout more efficiently. Use the empty-cells property and set the value to hide to remove empty data cells from view.

1. Create a style sheet which sets a 1px solid black table border for tables and cells:
   `border: 1px solid black;`

2. Add a declaration which hides empty table cells: `empty-cells: hide;`

3. Save and close the CSS file.

4. Open the HTML template and add a table to the `<body>` element with three rows and columns.

5. Fill some cells with data but leave at least three empty and add the `<link />` tag to your new style sheet.

6. Save the HTML file with a new name and open it in your web browser.

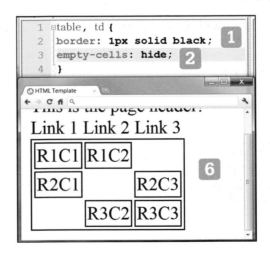

? **DID YOU KNOW?**

Hiding cells has no impact on table structure. It's different in this regard from absent cells which create uneven rows or columns.

? **DID YOU KNOW?**

The default value for empty cells is to be shown. If you do not want the empty cells in a table to be displayed as empty cells, you must set the empty-cells value to hide.

Top 10 HTML5 and CSS3 Problems Solved

Problem 1: I added an HTML element to my page but it's not showing on the screen

If an HTML document doesn't appear in the browser window as you expect, there isn't much which can go wrong, and HTML documents are fairly easy to troubleshoot.

1 Open the HTML document in a text editor.

2 Do a search for the element you're looking for using the text editor's search feature.

3 If the element is located in the search, check to make sure it has an opening and closing tag.

4 Be sure the element does *not* have a closing tag if it's an 'open' tag; they use a trailing slash instead.

5 Check the spelling of the element name and any properties or attributes against the WHATWG documentation.

6 Make any necessary corrections to the HTML markup and save the file, then reload it in the browser.

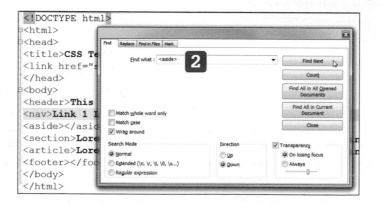

HOT TIP: Laziness with spelling isn't going to work in HTML (or any other scripting, programming or markup language, for that matter)! You *must* check your spelling and be sure it's accurate. The number one cause of failed code is misspelling. Be vigilant!

SEE ALSO: See Chapter 1's 'Bookmark reference sites' section for information on where to locate the WHATWG online.

Problem 2: My page doesn't look right on some computers

The way a page is displayed in a browser can be dependent on a lot of things. To solve the issue of variance between computers, there are several things to check. Ultimately how the page looks may be beyond your control, so don't panic too much if this happens.

1 Check to see if the web page you've created has Document Type Declaration.

2 Open the web browser which doesn't display the page correctly.

3 Check the version of the browser; generally, this is done in the Help, About menu option.

4 Check the web page of the browser manufacturer to determine if the latest version is being used.

5 If possible, try using a different browser on the same computer to determine if it's a standards-compliance problem with the browser.

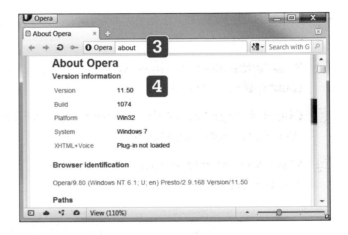

 HOT TIP: Internet Explorer (IE) is notorious for not keeping up with current standards prior to version 9. Most web designers either recommend using another browser right on the page as part of the content, or will craft special scripts and codes to make IE behave more like other browsers. If the browser having trouble is IE, check to see if the version is older than 9.0. If it is, the problem is probably a standards-compliance one and another browser is the easiest solution.

 ALERT: Some firewalls, especially for corporate computer network systems, can block pages which the company deems inappropriate for employees during working hours. Sometimes just portions of a page can be blocked.

Problem 3: I added some markup to content but it doesn't look any different in the browser

HTML markup may not be visible on your web page for a variety of reasons. When you find that your markup, in particular formatting markup, doesn't appear as expected in your browser, the following steps may help.

1 Open the HTML file in your text editor and search for the tag or element in question.

2 Check the spelling of the tag – remember, use US spellings for all attributes and values!

3 Check to ensure any attributes requiring enclosure in quotes have them.

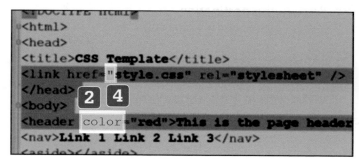

4 Ensure the quotes, if required, are *double* quotes ("), not *single* quotes (').

5 If the tag is an HTML5 tag, make sure the browser supports it by checking the version.

6 Finally, make sure the tag hasn't been deprecated.

► **SEE ALSO:** See the 'My page doesn't look right on some computers' section in this chapter for more information on checking browser versions.

? DID YOU KNOW?

There is a list of deprecated HTML tags listed on http://www.codehelp.co.uk/html/deprecated.html, with alternatives. Also, doing a search with a search engine such as Google will turn up many other places where a list of deprecated tags can be viewed. Bookmark your favourites as reference.

Problem 4: I added a hyperlink to my page but when I click it I get an error message page

Without question, the most common problems encountered in programming, scripting and markup are typographical error bugs. When you make a mistake in entering information, unexpected outcomes can result. In creating hyperlinks, having incorrect information can lead viewers away from your intended target, or into the vacuum of cyberspace!

1 Check the hyperlink and ensure the href attribute value is enclosed in double quotes (").

2 Be sure the destination reference is spelled correctly.

3 Make sure the destination reference is a full URL, including the http:// portion.

4 Ensure the suffix of the domain is correct (.com, .org, .info, .net, etc.).

5 Navigate to the page you want to link to and copy the URL from the address bar of your browser.

6 Use the editor's paste feature to paste the URL from your browser into the hyperlink's href value.

 DID YOU KNOW?

A URL is, by definition, a fully qualified uniform resource locator, which includes the protocol (http:// in our case), and a fully qualified domain name (for example, www. google.com).

 DID YOU KNOW?

Sometimes your browser is smart enough to know what you mean, and isn't rigidly adherent to what you typed. For example, if you put a hyperlink with an href value of http://www.gogle.com and click the link, your browser will understand you meant http://www.google.com/ and take you there instead of giving you an error message.

Problem 5: I put a submit button on my HTML form but nothing happens when I click it

An HTML form submit button needs more than the button on screen to function. When you click the button, the form must know where to send the data, and how the data should be sent. The action attribute tells the form where to send the information. The method attribute tells the form how to send the data.

1 Locate the submit button on your HTML document with your text editor.

2 Make sure the type attribute of the `<input  />` tag is set to "submit".

3 Locate the `<form>` element on the HTML document.

4 Make sure the action attribute is set to the correct data submission location and enclosed in double quotes.

5 Make sure the method attribute is set correctly and enclosed in double quotes.

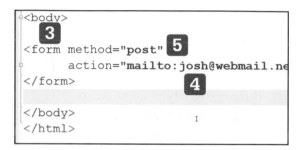

```
<body>
  3
<form method="post" 5
      action="mailto:josh@webmail.ne
</form>
          4
</body>
</html>
```

 ALERT: Only you will know whether the location to send the data to is accurately input, or if the correct method attribute setting is input.

? DID YOU KNOW?
Possible settings for the action attribute include an absolute URL, such as http://www.yourtargetdomain.com/, or a relative URL, such as ./yourtargetserverlocation/. See Chapter 4's 'Site navigation with relative URLs' for more information on using relative URLs, and Chapter 4's 'Use absolute URLs' for further details on the use of absolute URLs.

? DID YOU KNOW?
The method attribute tells the form how to send the data to the location specified in the action attribute. The two most common settings are post and get. The get method sends the data as HTTP name/value sets, while the post method sends the data as HTTP post. The details of these methods are well beyond the scope of this book, but much information is available online for free.

Problem 6: I positioned an element using the top, bottom, left or right property and now I can't see it

CSS3 positioning is simple and seems easy, but it can be quite tricky if the right measures aren't used or the right *amounts* of those measures aren't used. To find the element you can't see:

1 Open the style sheet you created with the property declaration on it.

2 Make sure the property is spelled correctly.

3 If the property is using fixed measures like pixels (px), change it to a percentage.

4 Check whether the values for the property are set in positive or negative numbers, and change to the opposite.

5 If all else fails, remove the declaration from the style sheet.

6 Save the style sheet and reload the page in the browser.

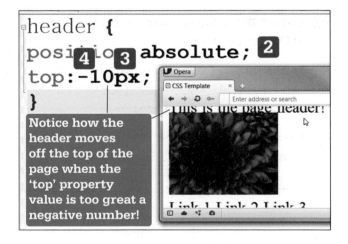

```
header {
    position: absolute;  2
    4    3
    top: -10px;
}
```

Notice how the header moves off the top of the page when the 'top' property value is too great a negative number!

HOT TIP: Spelling counts in coding! Be sure you have spelled the property declaration and all the values and settings correctly.

? DID YOU KNOW?

During the writing of this book, I encountered this very problem. By experimentation I discovered that using a negative value presented the problem, and by moving the number closer to 0 or using a positive value, I could position the element as desired.

Problem 7: I applied a CSS style to an element but it doesn't work

There can be a lot of reasons why a CSS declaration doesn't format an element properly. The layering effect of CSS can be problematic, if not accounted for. More than one rule applied to the same element can cause unexpected results. And there may be inherited formatting from the parent element involved.

1 Open the style sheet in your text editor and search for the selector for the element you want to format.

2 If the element selector is found, make sure the proper selector has been used.

3 Determine if the element which isn't formatted is a nested or child element, which may require a combinator.

4 Comment out the rule in the style sheet, and apply the rule in a `<style>` element in the HTML document.

5 If the internal style sheet fails, apply an inline style in the start tag for the element.

FREE

...ets (CSS 3)

	SELECTOR TYPES		
	Name	**Info**	**Example**
	Universal	Any element	* { font: 10px Arial; }
	Type	Any element of that type	h1 { text-decoration: underline; }
	Grouping	Multiple elements of different types	h1, h2, h3 { font-family: Verdana; }
	Class	Multiple elements of different types when you don't	.sampleclass { text-decoration: underline; }

🔥 **HOT TIP:** Combinators can be very powerful, but must be accurately coded to function. Be sure to check your spelling and you can use the CSS3 Selectors Reference Guide from W3Schools.com, located at http://www.w3schools.com/css3/css3_ref_selectors.asp.

? **DID YOU KNOW?**
There is a summary of CSS3 selectors on the quick reference guide for CSS3 from Veign.com.

Problem 8: My style sheet is lengthy and hard to read!

When working with either HTML or CSS, annotating code with comments is always a good idea. In addition, it may be helpful to dissect your documents into sections which make sense to you. For instance, keeping all the declarations for headings together in one section, or grouping the declarations according to sections of the web page they format. Putting each declaration on its own line may also help.

1 Open the style sheet with your text editor and immediately save it with a new name.

2 Figure out how you'd like to group the declarations together; jotting down the basics may help.

3 Locate the declarations to group together and cut and paste to move them to the new section(s).

4 Add CSS comments to the top of each section which explain what the section is for.

5 When all the declarations have been moved, save the style sheet again.

6 Test the style sheet to ensure you haven't missed anything by changing the `<link />` href value to the new sheet.

```css
/* This section formats headings and headers */
                              4
header {
font-face: arial, helvetica, sans-serif;
font-size: 16pt;                           3
color: slategray;
background-color: silver;
}

h1 {                              I
font-size: 14pt;
color: white;
background-color: gray;
}
```

? DID YOU KNOW?

If your style sheet works the way it should you can rename it to overwrite the existing one or change the link tag href values for any pages the style sheet formats. In general it will be easier to rename the style sheet since that will involve only one change. To preserve the old style sheet rather than overwrite it, simply rename it before changing the new style sheet's name. Be careful to preserve the existing style sheet before you alter it or you may cause unexpected formatting changes!

HOT TIP: Another way to clean up markup code is to place each declaration property on its own line, as seen in the screenshot.

! ALERT: Be careful to close the comments on your style sheet or you will comment out the declarations!

Problem 9: I formatted a font with CSS but it didn't change in the browser

If the CSS formatting you applied doesn't affect the web page as you expected, or at all, the problem could lie with the declaration in the CSS file. But it could also lie in the browser or even the computer itself.

1 Locate the declaration in the text editor and ensure the property is spelled correctly (font: value).

2 If the property is spelled correctly, make sure the value is also spelled correctly (the name of the font).

3 If the value is correct, make sure there is a semi-colon at the end of the declaration.

4 If the declaration has the semi-colon, make sure the declaration above has one.

5 If the CSS is correct, ensure the font is installed on the computer.

6 If the font is installed, check the version of the browser and update if necessary.

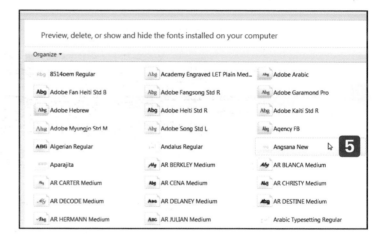

Preview, delete, or show and hide the fonts installed on your computer

Organize ▾

Abg 8514oem Regular	Abg Academy Engraved LET Plain Med...	Abg Adobe Arabic
Abg Adobe Fan Heiti Std B	Abg Adobe Fangsong Std R	Abg Adobe Garamond Pro
Abg Adobe Hebrew	**Abg** Adobe Heiti Std R	Abg Adobe Kaiti Std R
Abg Adobe Myungjo Std M	Abg Adobe Song Std L	Abg Agency FB
ABG Algerian Regular	Andalus Regular	Angsana New
Aparajita	**Abg** AR BERKLEY Medium	**Abg** AR BLANCA Medium
AR CARTER Medium	**Abg** AR CENA Medium	**Abg** AR CHRISTY Medium
AR DECODE Medium	**Abg** AR DELANEY Medium	**Abg** AR DESTINE Medium
AR HERMANN Medium	**Abg** AR JULIAN Medium	Arabic Typesetting Regular

SEE ALSO: See the 'My page doesn't look right on some computers' section earlier in this chapter for more information on checking browser versions.

 DID YOU KNOW?

Specific information on checking for installed fonts is dependent on your operating system. For Windows XP, the fonts reside in a folder called Fonts in the Windows/System 32 folder. For Windows Vista and Windows 7, the fonts folder is in the Windows/Fonts directory. Check your operating system's documentation, or search online, for information on where the font files are stored for other operating systems.

Problem 10: There's too much white space on my page

Controlling white space on a web page can help the reader find and read content more easily, but it's fairly easy to overdo. Be careful when using white space controls like margins and padding so you don't end up with vast areas of blank screen.

1 Open the style sheet for the HTML document with your text editor.

2 Locate the white space declarations for the elements with too much white space.

3 If there are declarations for margins and padding, decide which will best serve your content and site.

4 Comment out the declaration you decide not to use.

5 Save the style sheet and reload the web page to check the results.

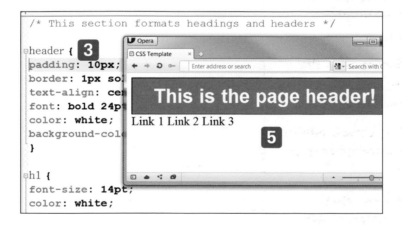

```
/* This section formats headings and headers */

header {  3
padding: 10px;
border: 1px so
text-align: ce
font: bold 24p
color: white;
background-col
}

h1 {
font-size: 14pt;
color: white;
```

This is the page header!

Link 1 Link 2 Link 3

? DID YOU KNOW?
Margins and padding are seldom necessary in the same declarations. The cumulative effect can be overwrought. Use one or the other for most applications.

? DID YOU KNOW?
By using only margins or only padding properties to create a single space among elements, your code will be cleaner and easier to read, as well as having a more professional quality.

Also available in the In Simple Steps series

9780273736806

9780273729136

9780273745419

9780273736844

9780273723530

9780273744139

9780273736820

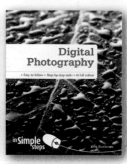

9780273723516

9780273736127

9780273744146

9780273745570

9780273746362

in Simple steps